Hidden Angels

an anthology of angels

D.M.M. PHD

Order this book online at www.trafford.com/07-1543
or email orders@trafford.com

Most Trafford titles are also available at major online book retailers.

Cover Design: Leon Soriano

Note for Librarians: A cataloguing record for this book is available from Library and Archives Canada at www.collectionscanada.ca/amicus/index-e.html

ISBN: 978-1-4251-3853-0

We at Trafford believe that it is the responsibility of us all, as both individuals and corporations, to make choices that are environmentally and socially sound. You, in turn, are supporting this responsible conduct each time you purchase a Trafford book, or make use of our publishing services. To find out how you are helping, please visit www.trafford.com/responsiblepublishing.html

Our mission is to efficiently provide the world's finest, most comprehensive book publishing service, enabling every author to experience success. To find out how to publish your book, your way, and have it available worldwide, visit us online at www.trafford.com/10510

www.trafford.com

North America & international
toll-free: 1 888 232 4444 (USA & Canada)
phone: 250 383 6864 ♦ fax: 250 383 6804 ♦ email: info@trafford.com

The United Kingdom & Europe
phone: +44 (0)1865 722 113 ♦ local rate: 0845 230 9601
facsimile: +44 (0)1865 722 868 ♦ email: info.uk@trafford.com

10 9 8 7 6 5

DEDICATION

Dedicated to my loving and ever caring family, and especially to my son Albert, who once asked me, "What are Angels?" Not being happy with my reply, I promised to look it up. I hope that this is a better answer.

PROLOGUE

Since time immemorial, mankind has believed in the concept of certain forces and entities that have been protective and kind towards human beings. From time to time, as evidenced in the Bible, either wholly, or semi-supernatural, beings have come to his assistance. Much of the knowledge concerning Angels has been lost or veiled, owing to the ever present danger of Man inclining towards the establishment of a Cult of Angels, rather than concentrating and devoting himself to the worship of the One True G-d. This is substantiated by the fact that it is difficult to find information about the Old Testament Angels. Many are not named, and those scholars who seem to be knowledgeable tend to refer whoever is interested in the topic to encyclopedias which convey little information on the subject.

We are told in 2nd *Kings 3:21* that the new king, Manasseh, was a wicked king and re-established the worship of idols: "and worshipped all the host of heaven and served them." One school of thought maintains that the "host" meant the sun, moon and planets. Others believe this to mean the Angelic host of heaven and from thence we arrive at the injunction not to worship Angels or even to invoke them.

In its simplest form, the Biblical term for Angel is derived from the word "Malach", which means "Messenger". In addition, the specific name borne by each Angel obtains further significance by the addition of G-d's name. For example, Micha-el means who is like unto G-d. While Rapha-el means G-d has healed. Our impression of what Angels look like has been largely distorted by artists who have portrayed Angels as white robed winged beings with human features. The Fifteenth Century (CE.) Flemish artist, Roger Van der Weyden, painted many of his Angels with bald heads. In the Bible, Angels are described as appearing to man in human form of extraordinary beauty and are not always immediately recognized as Angels. It is for this reason that students of the Bible are often confused as to whether a particular messenger is human or supernatural and whether it is an Angel or G-d who is speaking. What some scholars fail to realize, as a result of this ambiguity, is that the Almighty speaks through his messengers, the Angels.

Throughout the Bible, we find Angels flying through the air and having the power to become invisible. They disappear in sacrificial fire (1st *Kings 18:32*) and appear in the flames of the burning bush set before Moses (*Exodus 3:2*). Being celestial, they are pure and bright, and often are encompassed by light or fire.

In *Genesis 3:21* we are told that the Almighty made coats of skins for Adam and his wife and clothed them. Prior to this, they had worn celestial garments of light, as do the Angels. From this, one might infer that Adam and Eve were initially celestial, as opposed to earthly beings. The reference to new garments of skin has been interpreted as denoting human flesh, the very substance that presently covers our bodies. This human skin was given to Adam and Eve so that they could adapt to the great changes that their expulsion from Eden would introduce. According to the Zohar, Angels also have to put on an earthly garment when they descend to earth. Without it, they can neither remain nor be understood on this earthly plain.

As Angels are incorporeal, they are not subject to the limitations of time and space. Though supernatural, they can assume human form, bearing drawn swords or other weapons of Destruction (*Genesis 3:24*). In the Bible some ride on horseback, one carries an ink-horn by his side and is clothed in fine linen (*Ezekiel 9:2*), while yet another has the appearance of burnished brass (*Ezekiel 1:7*). Each Biblical reference gives a different description. This is only fitting, since each manifestation is intended to be seen by a particular individual, whose interpretation must, of necessity, be uniquely personal.

According to Kabalistic teachings, there are four separate, mystical worlds. Angels govern the World of Formation, or the Yetziratic World. Arch Angels (i.e. Chief Angels), on the other hand, govern the World of Beriyah or the World of Creation. Because Angels can perform only one kind of task at a time, no Angel can undertake the task of another, but he may carry out several within his mandate. The Talmud, (*Bereshith Rabah, section 1*), asserts that no Angel can perform two things at one time. It is for this reason that three Angels were sent to Abraham: one to announce to Sarah the birth of Isaac, the other to destroy Sodom and Gomorra, and the third to save Lot and his family. Although not specified, the names of these three Angels may be deduced by using Gematria. Gematria is a system widely employed in the Kabala. It is based on the relative numerical value of words and phrases, which are equal, and therefore explanatory of each other, since every letter in the Hebrew Alphabet has a numerical value. By using this system, taking "Lo three men [stood by him]" (*Genesis 18:2*), we are able to deduce that the three men were the Arch Angels Michael, Gabriel and Raphael:

שלשה	והנה	
5+300+30+300	**5+50+5+6**	**=701**

ורפאל	גבריאל	מיכאל	אלו
30+1+80+200+6	**30+1+10+200+2+3**	**30+1+20+10+40**	**6+30+1**
		=701	

Genesis 19:1 does not describe the remaining two Angels, Gabriel and Raphael, as men but as fully fledged Angels "And there came two Angels to Sodom at even." The Archangel Michael had already fulfilled his mission with the announcement that Sarah would bare a son and the remaining tasks were to be completed by Gabriel and Raphael.

Through the centuries, the study of Angelology has become blurred by the many different interpretations of the functions which certain Angels perform. At one stage, the use of a particular Angelic name denoted a precise definition of a Yetziratic function. With time, this knowledge (which was never recorded, but passed down orally from Master to disciple), was lost, or became confused and thus unusable. It is for this reason that so much contradiction exists in the study of Kabala today.

The Kabala tells us that there are ten Sephirot. The best rendering of the word Sephirot is "Numerical Emanations", "Divine Attributes", or "Manifestations of the Absolute". Since Angels are guardians of the Sephirotic functions assigned to them (see Tables i, ii and iii), it is quite natural to accept the concept of Guardian Angels in terms of individual and even national experience. This concept will be dealt with in greater detail in the chapter on Guardian Angels.

One of the many functions served by Angels is to be present at human gatherings. The meeting of a number of people will usually produce a spirit which connects and evokes the Angel who will preside over the convocation. For instance, Seraphim and Chashmalim are present at prayer meetings. Occasionally, if the balance and merit of those participating are right, the Archangels Raphael and Haniel (the spirits of healing and wisdom and understanding) will descend upon the group of people attempting, through meditation, to make contact with the spirit of knowledge. This being accomplished, the holy spirit of Gabriel then descends upon the group, and those who are attuned will become aware of the Shechina or Divine Presence. In a lighter vein, Cherubim and Ishim are to be found at such exciting events as football matches or baseball games.

Many Angels govern different parts of the universe. One has control over one sphere, while another is in charge of a different planet or heavenly body. The sun, moon, earth, sea, fire, wind, light or seasons each have their own controlling Angel, who derives his name from that which he guards. So, for example, the angel guarding Venus is called Negah; the Angel of fire is Nuriel; while the Angel of Light is Uriel.

Although highly evolved, Angels have no axis of consciousness and, unlike man, no will of their own. In fact, it is firmly established in the Talmud (*Sanhedrin 93a*) that the righteous are greater than Angels. Angelic beings cannot evolve spiritually any further. They are fixed in their perfection, and operate in the lower worlds without choice or any possibility of evolving further, for they have already reached their fulfillment.

This places man in a unique and privileged position. His role is growth which eventually evolves into perfection. If it were not so, creation would be like a machine with no awareness other than that of the Almighty to appreciate its beauty and ingenuity. Herein lies man's uniqueness:

"We know that we know that we are known by the Knower." (Source unknown.)

Angels are also given charge of the twelve signs of the Zodiac. For example, according to the Zohar (*Shmot 78a*), the passage in *Exodus 19:1* "In the third month, when the children of Israel were gone forth out of the land of Egypt" refers to Uriel, the celestial Archangel who has sway over the third month. He is referred to again in *Exodus 4:24-26* when "The Lord met him [Moses] and sought to kill him" because Moses had neglected to circumcise his son Gershom. Moses' wife Zipporah redeemed the situation by swiftly circumcising her son with a sharp stone.

Uriel, the Angel of Light, is in charge of three hundred and sixty five myriad of camps of Angels. All possess the same number of keys of light which is the color of electrum. This light issues from their supernal sphere and although it is divided into two, it remains one light. The first light is reserved for the righteous, and is the light of Wisdom and Understanding, while the second light is one which sparkles for all mankind. The light is known as the "Twins". It is therefore ordained that the constellation of Gemini (i.e. Twins) rules the month of Sivan - the month the Torah was given. In its usual veiled manner, the Zohar here appears to intimate that the wisdom of the Torah is available to all, but that the inner wisdom it contains is reserved only for the righteous few. We are fortunate indeed that today many people believe that the advent of the coming of the Messiah is close at hand and that the wisdom of the Kabala will therefore be unveiled to all who seek its knowledge.

In the Kabala, it is stated that in the beginning the Almighty taught the secrets of creation to the highest Archangels, who formed a supreme council in his Celestial Court. We are also told that the laws governing Creation are based on the ten Sephirot.

To each Sephirah was ascribed an Archangel, as well as the Order of Angels over which he held dominion. The Zohar states:

> "After the Sephirot and for their use,
> G-d made the throne (that is the World of
> Creation) with four legs and six steps.....
> For this throne and its service he formed
> Ten Angelic Hosts (the World of Formation),
> Malachim, Arelim, Chaioth, Ophanim,
> Chashmalim Elim, (Cherubim), Elohim,
> Bnei Elim, Ishim and Seraphim. For their
> service, again, he made Samael
> and his legions (the World of Action) who are,
> as it were, the clouds upon which the Angels

> ride in their descent on the earth, and serve,
> as it were, for their horses. Hence it is written
> "Behold the Lord rideth upon a swift cloud and
> shall come to Egypt"
>
> *(Isaiah 19:1)*

Angels are exactly what their name implies – messengers; no more and no less. Especially over the past two millennia, Angels have mistakenly been regarded as having supernatural powers, and as being divided into two distinct camps: The forces of good at endless war with the forces of evil. This is not the case at all.

Throughout the Midrash, the Lord's Ministering Angels are often portrayed as His counselors. Before creating Adam, the Lord's words, "Let Us make man" are taken as meaning that He was actually addressing the Angels to attain their opinion.

The Angels split into different factions, either opposing or favoring the creation of man. the Angel of Kindness affirmed in favor, for man would practise kindness. The Angel of Truth (sometimes identified as Amitiel) protested, since man would be full of falsehood. The Angel of Love, who is not mentioned by name in the Kabala, approved because humans would have a great potential for expressing love. Michael, the Angel of Righteousness, voted for man's creation, for man would perform acts of righteousness. The Angel of Peace (Although unnamed some writers say there are many Angels of Peace notably Mahasiah and Lehachia to name but two) protested, since man would be full of strife, and would always wish to wage war.

Even the Angel of Earth, some commentators list as many as seven Angels but again in this Midrash he is not mentioned by name, rebelled in his protest by refusing to give Gabriel any dust from which to create man. He went on to list how man would ruin the earth in his thoughtlessness and bad conservation methods and if the Almighty wanted earth to create man He would have to take it Himself and not use the intermediary of an Angel.

Finally, even the Torah protested, arguing that man's life span would be short and filled with tribulations. He would most certainly sin, and would constantly try the Almighty's forbearance.

The Lord prevailed over the objections of both the Angels and the Torah, and decided in favor of man's creation. His final words were, "I am kind and long suffering, and am ready to create man, despite his faults".

To some readers this might pose a contradiction and one might very well ask two questions: "Is this not putting limitations on the Almighty? As the Omniscient Creator of the Universe why should He be placed in a situation by something He has the power to rectify?" The answer lies in the Mystical lessons of the Kabala which teach that had the Almighty created man perfect, it would have been too easy for him. Instead, man must undergo thousands of trials and tribulations and learn countless lessons before attaining perfection.

The Midrash, the Hebrew exposition of the Old Testament, goes on to state that before G-d created man, the Angels asked what kind of creature he would be. They were told that man's intellect would be superior to theirs, and to prove it the Creator of the Universe brought all the animals before the Angels and asked them to name each one. Not one Angel was capable of doing so, and watched while Adam correctly named all the animals, first in Hebrew, and then in each of the other seventy languages which he intuitively knew. The reason that the Angels were not able to name the animals is because each Angel is created to fulfill only one mission or task at a time. They are therefore single-minded, and possess no knowledge of any characteristic outside of their own.

In many of the Psalms, Angels are portrayed as G-d's choristers, seemingly doing little else but singing His praise. This is mainly because the Psalms were written as a guide for man to praise his maker, and to follow the example set by the Creator's Ministering Angels.

After having experienced the great miracle of the parting of the Red Sea [correctly the Sea of Reeds], the Children of Israel were so filled with faith that the Holy Spirit rested on them, and they broke out in the well-known song, "Shira" (*Exodus 15:1-18*). A Midrashic legend tells us that, while the Egyptians were drowning in the Red Sea, the Angels in Heaven wanted to join in and sing "Shira" to the Almighty. They were forbidden to do so, however, since the Israelites were still crossing the sea in mortal fear. On seeing the last Hebrew cross safely, the Angels wished to take up their song, but the Lord once again refused, saying: "How can I let you sing while my creatures, the Egyptians, are drowning? My mercy includes all beings. Only after my sons sing Shira will you be allowed to follow suit". Moses first sang, and he was followed by all the Israelite men. Once they had finished, Miriam took up her cymbals and chanted the Shira with all the womenfolk. Knowing that the Angels would complain, Miriam graciously allowed the Angels to sing with her.

Singing praises to the Almighty is a pleasurable duty which is undertaken by all Angels. According to the Zohar (*Vayesheb 188b-189a*), every Angel is accorded his own special service to perform before his Master. Some serve as messengers, and take charge of guiding man, while others chant praises to the Holy One, blessed be He. However, no matter what their charge, there is not one Angel that does not sing the Lord's praise. As soon as night falls, three hosts, consisting of myriads of Angels, range themselves in three quarters of the entire universe. Under the chieftainship of a sacred Chaya, the chanting continues until daybreak. As soon as daylight arrives, the children of Israel take up the song and offer praises three times a day. The same sacred Chaya that took charge of the chanting at night presides over the litanies by day. It is imperative that every Angel be present at all convocations where praise is sung to the Almighty.

The Kabala tells us that there are 4 Universes. They are Atzilut-Emanation, Beriyah-Creation, Yetzirah-Formation and Asiyah-Making. *Isaiah* 43:7 states "All that is created in My Name, for My Glory [Atzilut], I have created it [Beriyah], I have formed it [Yetzirah] and I have made it [Asiyah].

The highest Universe is Atzilut, meaning nearness or emanation. This is the Universe of the 10 Sephirot [Table i].

In Hebrew the word Sefer ספר , meaning book, has the same root as the word Sefirah ספירה . Sefer is masculine while Sefirah is feminine. There are ten Sephirot, or emanations out of nothing [Ayin Sof- the unknowable]. They are solely figures of speech and should not be taken literally because they are mere symbols of a spiritual reality above the bounds of human consciousness. Their descriptions endeavor to convey something of the beyond and should one become fixated with the image itself, one entirely misses the point.

Contemporary students of the Kabala should not attempt to anthropomorphize each emanation or attribute but rather realize that man was created in the image of G-d and therefore the Sephirot are the Divine Attributes which man should strive to attain.

In its description of Creation, the first Chapter of Genesis mentions the word Elohim [G-d] thirty two times. It states "G-d said" 10 times corresponding to the 10 Sefirot. Actually the first "G-d said" is purported to be *Genesis 1:1* "In the Beginning *G-d created* the heavens and the Earth". Although the words "G-d said" are not actually mentioned here they are implied and understood.

The number thirty two also alludes to the twenty two letters of the Hebrew Alphabet, or Aleph Beth, plus the 10 Sephirot. This is described more fully in Sepher Yetzira or The Book of Formation.

In the Bahir the 10 Sephirot are referred to as the 10 Utterances. The Sephirot are mentioned in just about all discourses of the Kabala and it is essential for any student to understand them in all their complexity. The Sephirot exist neither in Space or Time but represent an inner divine reality- the 10 within the ONE.

The first three Sephirot are so profound that man can never begin to fathom them but must be content in the knowledge that he is able to fully understand the ensuing seven Sephirot, which are more at the level of his comprehension. Many Kabalists often refer to these seven Sephirot as Zeir Anpin.

KETER - CROWN

The first Sephira is KETER or the CROWN of the Ayin Sof [the Unknowable]. It is also the crown of Adam Kadmon, the Primordial man, who was created in the image of G-d. It is he who was seen in the Chariot Vision of *Ezekiel 1:1*. It represents the primal stirrings of intent within Ayin Sof and the desire to commence His wonderful and varied Creation.

Keter-Crown is the starting point of the cosmic process. Since the Sephirot are portrayed as a symbolic body of a kingly figure, it is only fitting that the highest manifestation of the emerging spiritual body should begin with a crown to adorn the head. Most Kabbalists portray a beautiful vision of the Ayin Sof whose head is adorned each morning with the letters and words which form the prayers of the pious and righteous of this world. This daily coronation rite which takes place in Heaven as well as on Earth is central to the ancient Merkavah [Chariot] traditions and the position of Keter-Crown as the head of the Sephirot reflects the influence of Merkavah mysticism in Kabala. We should not, however, loose sight of the fact that the word Keter also means circle, hence the crown, which encircles the head. Sepher Yetzira tells us that the Sephirot are a great circle, "Their end tied to their beginning and their beginning tied to their end."

Keter-Crown represents G-d's will, the source of the Torah. "The study of the Torah encompasses all". The crown, worn above the head, represents Hochmah-Wisdom and Binah-Understanding. Both the latter are aspects of conscious mentality. The Torah is wisdom and is therefore the "head" of creation.

Some might say that the Torah was only created to rectify creation as it already exists. If this were so the Torah would have been created after the earth, instead the Torah was the blue print of creation and therefore preceded it. The Yetziratic Angels of Chaioth Ha Qodesh whose Prince is Metatron, the Angel of the Presence, are guardians of this Sephira.

HOCHMAH -WISDOM

Out of the depths of Nothingness shines the Primordial Point of HOCHMAH, WISDOM. Nothing can give rise to something and yet the move from Keter to Hochmah was the initial step in the primal process. It was a transition from nothingness to being - from pure potential to the first point of real existence.

It was through Wisdom that "in the beginning" G-d created the world. The Kabala says that Creation and Revelation are twin Processes - existence and language, the real and the theoretical all emerge from the hidden mind of G-d, the Creator. Because Hochmah is the primal point of existence, it is symbolized by the letter yod - י, the smallest of all the letters and the first point from which all the other letters would be written. It is said that the entire Torah, its commentaries and in fact all of human wisdom is contained in a single yod. The upper point of the yod points upward toward Keter which in itself is designated by the letter aleph א or the divine name EHYEH אהיה, meaning I AM. This word was disclosed to Moses at the burning bush.

The Almighty encompasses all things including space and time. He is not encompassed by them. In fact to a mystic space and time do not exist on the higher plane. Hochmah-Wisdom, which we now know is the concept of The Beginning without end, was created even before space and time.

Eternity is the veritable ultimate concealment, since our minds cannot penetrate infinite time nor can they fathom the timelessness of true eternity. The "concealment" mentioned here alludes to Keter-Crown which is above and also the source of Hochmah-Wisdom. Guarding the Sephira of Hochmah-Wisdom are the Yetziratic Angels, the Ophanim, whose Prince is the Beriatic Archangel, Ratziel.

Hochmah-Wisdom now expands into the circle of Binah and plants a seed into the next Sephira, Binah-Understanding.

BINAH - UNDERSTANDING

BINAH-UNDERSTANDING, is like a Divine Womb, sown by Hochmah's seed of Holiness by which Binah then gives birth to the seven lower Sephirot who in turn give rise to the rest of Creation, which is at the opposite pole to the Creator. The Creator gives existence while creation accepts it. Before creation could be brought into existence the concept of differentiation had to be brought into being, which is the essence of Binah-Understanding. Binah shares the same root as Bein [between]. It is through understanding that the mind differentiates between one thing and another. So understanding is more commonly accepted as a concept of differentiation.

Our sages maintain that in Understanding is "counsel, strength, knowledge and the fear of G-d". Counsel by deeds of kindness; Strength which we must have to diligently perform these deeds; Knowledge is Truth and that which recognizes the truth; the Fear of G-d is the Treasury of the Torah.

When G-d added the letter Heh ה To Abraham's name, He gave him dominance over the final parts of the body, namely two eyes, two ears and the sexual organ. Abraham אברהם, numerically equals, 248 which traditionally are the number of parts in the human body.

Heh equals 5, alluding to the five levels of the soul which were thus automatically achieved by Abraham. The five levels of the Soul are:

Sefirah	*Universe*	*Soul Level*
Keter-Crown	Adam Kadmon	Yechidah-Uniqueness
Hochmah-Wisdom	Atzilut-Nearness	Chaya-Vitality
Binah-Understanding	Beriyah-Creation	Neshamah-Breath
The next 6 Sephirot	Yetzirah-Formation	Ruach-Wind, Spirit
Malchut-Kingship	Asiyah-Making	Nefesh-Soul

There are two Hehs in the Tetragrammaton YUD HEH VAV HEH. The first Heh corresponds to the Sefirah, Binah-Understanding and this is the "Hand" that G-d gives to man namely the reward of the World to Come. The final Heh is the Sefirah of Malchut-Kingship and this is the "Hand" He gives man so that he should be able to receive this great reward.

The Angels who are given the task of guarding Binah-Understanding are the Aralim whose leader is the Archangel Tsaphqiel, the Contemplation of G-d.

The triad of the higher Sephirot, Keter-Crown, Hochmah-Wisdom and Binah-Understanding, cannot be understood by man. They represent the head of the Divine and therefore are more hidden than the offspring of Binah-Understanding which are the next seven Sephirot.

DAAT - KNOWLEDGE

When making a diagram of the Sephirot many Kabalists add an eleventh Sephira in the central column which usually has four Sephirot. When the quasi Sephira, DAAT-KNOWLEDGE is added making the number of Sefirot

5, it brings out the significance of the letter Nun. By multiplying 5 by 10 we get 50, the numerical value of Nun. It is through Wisdom (Hochmah) and Understanding (Binah) that we achieve Knowledge (Daat). Daat descends to become the Sephira Tiferet-Beauty. The archangel Uriel, the Prince of Peace is the one associated with Tiferet-Beauty and it is through "understanding" [Binah] that "peace" will come to the world and man will realize the "beauty" [Tiferet] of existence.

HESED - MERCY

HESED-MERCY, is better translated as LOVING KINDNESS [Its color is White]. The two Sephirot Hesed-Mercy and Gevurah-Judgment are opposite poles of the Divine.

Free flowing Love and Strict Judgment are both essential for the world to function properly. Hesed-Mercy is akin to, or parallels water which flows freely from a high place as does Hesed-Mercy.

Hesed-Mercy/Loving Kindness is said to be below "Spirit' which is Binah-Understanding. We base this on the verse "And the spirit of G-d hovered upon the face of the waters". [*Genesis* 1:2] It is the first of the lower seven Sephirot which correspond to the seven days of creation. As such it is the primary building block of creation. To quote the *Psalms* "I have said that the world is built on "Hesed;" and again in *Psalm 136:6* "To him who stretched out the earth above the waters for his mercy (Hesed) endures forever. Because the concept of Chesed-Loving Kindness begins the Torah on the first day of creation, it is through Loving Kindness that man is initiated into the Torah.

The Chashmalim, headed by the Archangel, Tsadqiel, fittingly named the Benevolence of G-d, are the Angels whose duty it is to guard the Sephira of Mercy.

GEVURAH - STRENGTH

GEVURAH-STRENGTH is also known as Din [Law] or Judgment. [Its color is Red] Din is the purgative power of Judgment. The concept of Gevurah is Restraint. When it is said that Strength is Restraint it refers to the teaching from Perke Avot 4:1 "Who is strong, he who can restrain his urge." Man should and can restrain his nature and obviously so can G-d. G-d's nature is obviously to do good, but when he restrains it the result is that man is performing evil. The Sefirah of Gevurah-Strength is therefore seen as the source of evil.

Let us now consider the Hebrew letter Chet ח which is the final letter of the word Ruach רוח. Here the letter alludes to the three directions or winds, which are closed. They are South, East and West, each corresponding to the Sephirot Chesed-Loving Kindness Tiferet-Beauty and Yesod-Foundation. The only open direction Is North, corresponding to Gevurah-Strength. North is associated with evil and is said to be open since the existence of evil opens the door for free will. We are told that Samael, the Severity of G-d, heads the Yetziratic Angels, the fiery Seraphim, who sternly guard this Sephira.

As a passing thought, Gevurah-Strength is not all evil because The Archangel Gabriel, the Strength of G-d stands on the left of G-d and is the Officer in charge of all the Holy Forms to the left of the Holy One.

TIFERET - BEAUTY

TIFERET-BEAUTY is the color of Green. Ideally a balance must be found for Love and Judgment. This is symbolized by the central sefirah, Tiferet-Beauty, which is also called Rachamim or Compassion. If Judgment is not tempered by love through compassion, it lashes out and destroys life. Here lies the Sitra Ahara or the Other Side. Tiferet is the 'trunk' of the sephirotic body. It is called Heaven, Sun, King and even The Holy One.

Chesed seeks, Gevurah hides while Tiferet finds. The Hassidics say that Tiferet-Beauty is the quality of Truth which is spelled Aleph Mem Tav אמת. In Hebrew Aleph is the first letter of the alphabet, Tav is the last while Mem is considered to be the middle letter. While all things are not all separately true, truth does lie in the integration of all the composite parts from beginning to end, including all that is in between. The word "Tiferet" appears many times in the psalms and in the liturgy of many Hebrew religious services.

The Malachim, headed by their Archangel Michael spread their vigilance over the aspects of this Sephira.

NETZACH - VICTORY

Water is often mentioned in the Bible. Ice on the other hand, being frozen water indicates the concept of water once it is transformed into a state of permanence. The word NETZACH - VICTORY also has the connotation of permanence and eternity, alluding to man's permanent state in the world to come where "the righteous sit, delighting in the radiance of the Devine Presence or Shechina". The Angels seen by *Ezekiel 1:22* are always in that same state of permanence "for above their heads was a likeness of fearsome ice."
Netzach-Victory and Hod-Splendor are the 2 sefirot involved in prophesy and divine vision. This is because they are both the lowest of the Sefirot that, for example, touch the ground. When one ascends on high, they are the first Sefirot that can be reached and thus they are the source of prophesy.

Governing the Sephira of Netzach-Victory are the Yetziratic Angels, the Elohim also known as Tarshishim. Their Beriatic leader is the Archangel Haniel, the Grace of G-d. He is fittingly named for it is by the Grace of G-d that victory is accomplished.

HOD - GLORY

Netzach-Victory and HOD - GLORY also referred to as Splendor represent the feet of Zeir Anpin [the six sefirot before Malchut-Kingdom]. Netzach-Victory is depicted with the foot raised upward while Hod-Splendor is lowered downwards. These two sefirot represent the up-down directions. The head of Zeir Anpin is usually depicted to the East while the feet are to the West. The left foot [Hod-Glory] inclines to the north, the side of Gevurah-Strength which is the Source of Judgment and Evil. It is from Hod-Glory that evil is nourished. "For the imagination of man's heart is evil from his youth" [*Genesis 8:21*] and it does not incline in any other direction but to the left for it is already accustomed to being there.
There is a brighter and more positive side to Hod-Glory and that is EMPATHY. The flow of Hod-Glory is responsible for the creation of space in any relationship, providing the listener to pause and empathize. One cannot empathize with a sick friend unless one has experienced being sick and knowing exactly what it is like. Empathy is the very essence of a caring relationship.

Hod-Glory as Empathy, tempers the force of Netzach-Victory, which if allowed to go unchecked, can create distance rather than closeness. When holding back and accepting adversity or pain, we display a characteristic of Hod-Empathy.

We should never entertain negative feelings such as anger or the feeling of being cheated but rather, through the aspects of Hod-Glory, reshape the experience into a more meaningful, positive and active essence. The basis of Hod-Glory allows the creation of a neutral and accepting attitude and the manifestation of a more positive inclination.

Aron, the brother of Moses is considered one of the greatest mediators of the Bible. He brought peace between people because he used the key to mediation which is Hod-Empathy. It is for this reason that he is considered the epitome of the Sefirah of Hod-Empathy.

The guardians of Hod-Glory are the Bnei Elohim whose leader is none other than the Healer of G-d, Raphael. We cannot show empathy for a sick person unless we ourselves have experienced illness and have been healed through the grace of Raphael. In fact we can only empathize when we ourselves have undergone a similar experience.

YESOD - FOUNDATION

Souls are born through the union of YESOD-FOUNDATION and Malchut-Kingdom. It is for this reason that Yesod-Foundation is known as the "foundation of all souls." Here lies a conundrum. It is also said that the seventh Sefirah of the lower Sephirot, Malchut-Kingdom, represented by the Sabbath, is the sustainer of all souls. The answer is simple. While Malchut-Kingdom is the womb of all souls, Yesod-Foundation only functions to create souls in conjunction with Malchut-Kingdom. Yesod-Foundation mainly operates on the Sabbath.

Yesod-Foundation corresponds to the sixth day of creation the day on which Adam was created. He only attained the full aspect of his soul on the First Sabbath. He thus would have been permitted to eat from the Tree of Knowledge on that Sabbath, but instead he did not wait and ate there from on the sixth day.

Usually Yesod-Foundation is depicted as the ninth Sefirah, but as Malchut-Kingdom is considered the seventh because it pertains to the Sabbath, Yesod-Foundation is now thought of as the eighth Sefirah. As Yesod-Foundation cannot function without Malchut-Kingdom, it is analogous to the male sexual organ, which cannot reproduce without the female counterpart.

Ritual Circumcision is performed on the eighth day because it initiates the child into the eighth level. The number 7 represents the perfection of the physical creation, exemplified by the Sabbath. 8 is the level above the physical which is the transcendental. In the Sefirot the transcendental corresponds to the level of Binah-Understanding. Circumcision rectifies the male organ and therefore makes man more worthy of understanding Binah-Understanding.

The Angel of circumcision is Elijah and the baby who is being circumcised is placed on an empty chair called the Chair of Elijah so as to symbolically represent the child's reception by Elijah as a future son of the covenant. It is also said that should any barren married lady of child bearing age sit upon the Chair of Elijah, she will fall pregnant within a year of having done so.

The Sephira of Yesod-Foundation has the Cherubim headed by Gabriel as its guardians. Gabriel means the Strength of G-d and no plan or edifice can exist without a strong foundation.

MALCHUT - KINGDOM.

MALCHUT-KINGDOM or SOVEREIGNTY is also known as the Shechina, the Presence of G-d. The Six Sefirot of Zeir Anpin represent the 6 directions. Malchut-Kingdom is their center point. In this connotation, Malchut-Kingdom represents the Sabbath which is here seen as the middle of the week, preceded and followed by three days. In other words, everyday should be used to act righteously and praise the Lord.

Malchut-Kingdom completes the cycle which commenced with a moment of inspiration and finds its actualization in the real world. Without Malchut-Kingdom we would possess thoughts, but we would never be able to actualize them.

Malchut literally means Sovereignty. Malchut-Kingdom is a passive but powerful state of being. More importantly it is a more active and final state of actualization. Malchut-Kingdom gives us a glimpse of the divine sovereignty of the world. Malchut is the sovereign state that exists within each of us. It is through our thoughts, speech and behavior that others can glance at the sovereign power that rules within us. Therefore it is only natural that the guardian

Angels of this Sephira are the Ishim whose leader is Sandalphon, the manifest Messiah.

Malchut-Kingdom is the source of all the other Sefirot. The concept of Keter-Crown is that of purpose while Malchut-Kingdom is fulfillment. Together they define the spiritual dimension we call Soul. Creation's ultimate purpose involves motivation from below and in this respect Malchut-Kingdom is dominant.

TABLE I

THE TEN SEPHIROT

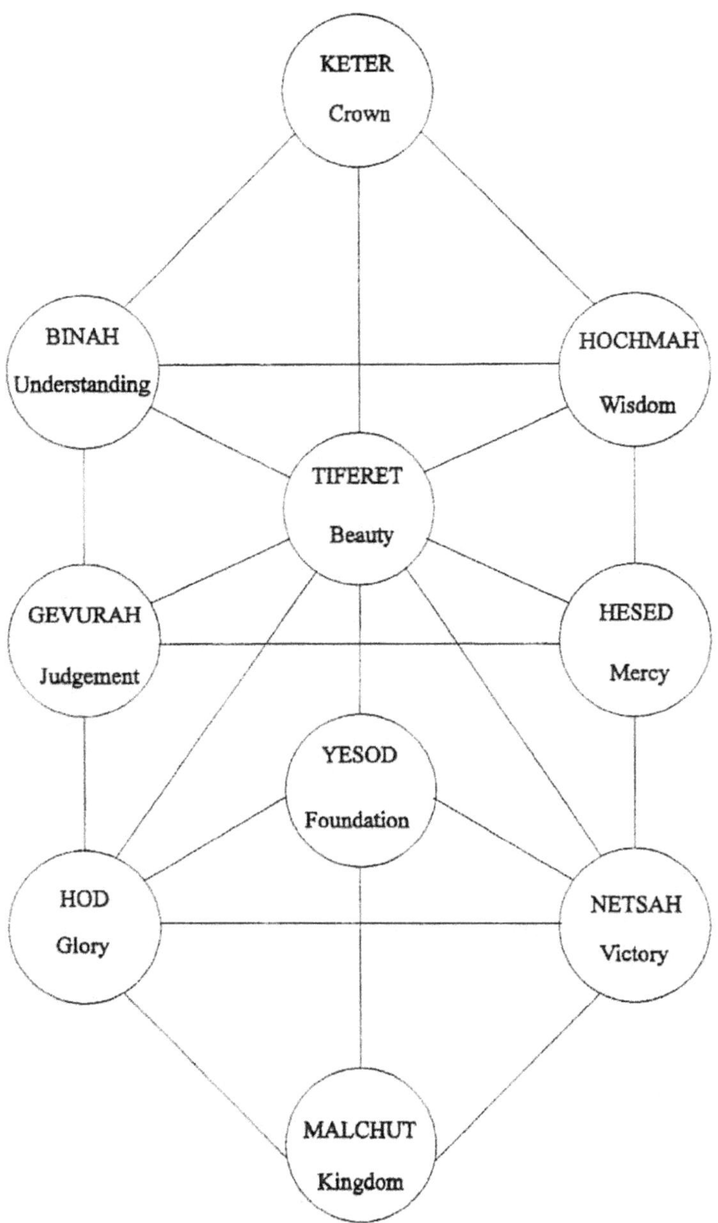

TABLE II

TEN CLASSES OF YETZIRATIC ANGELS

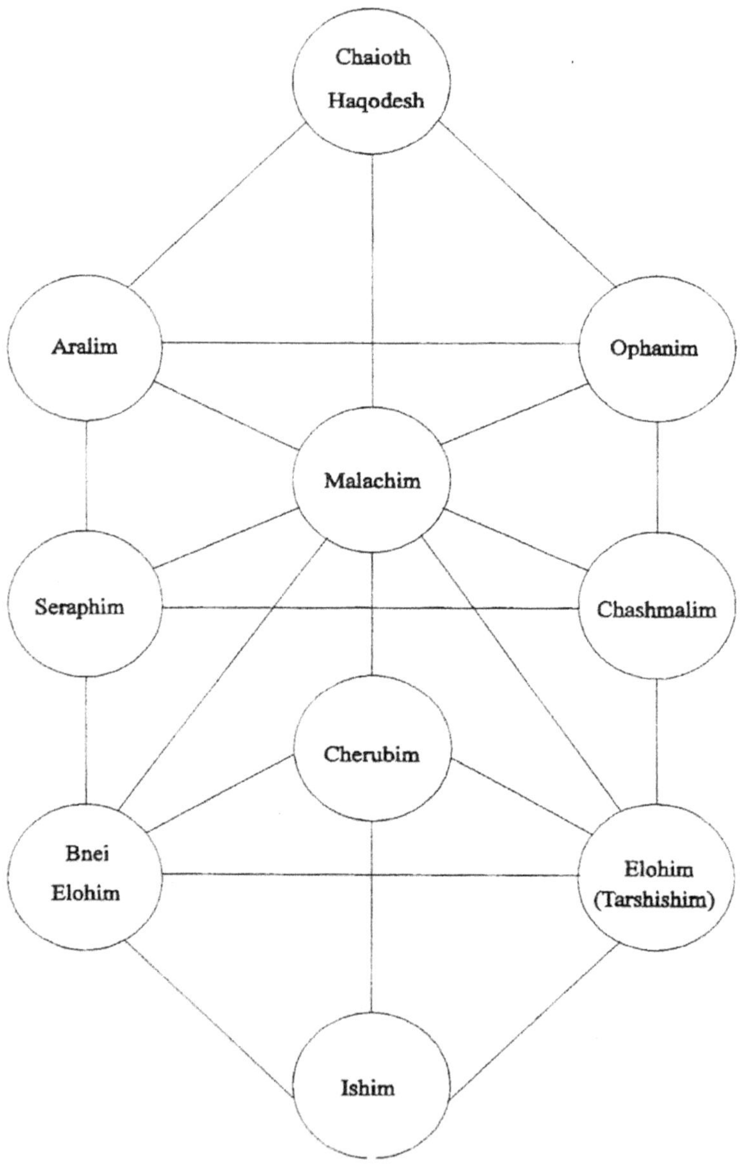

TABLE III

ARCH ANGELS OF BERIYAH

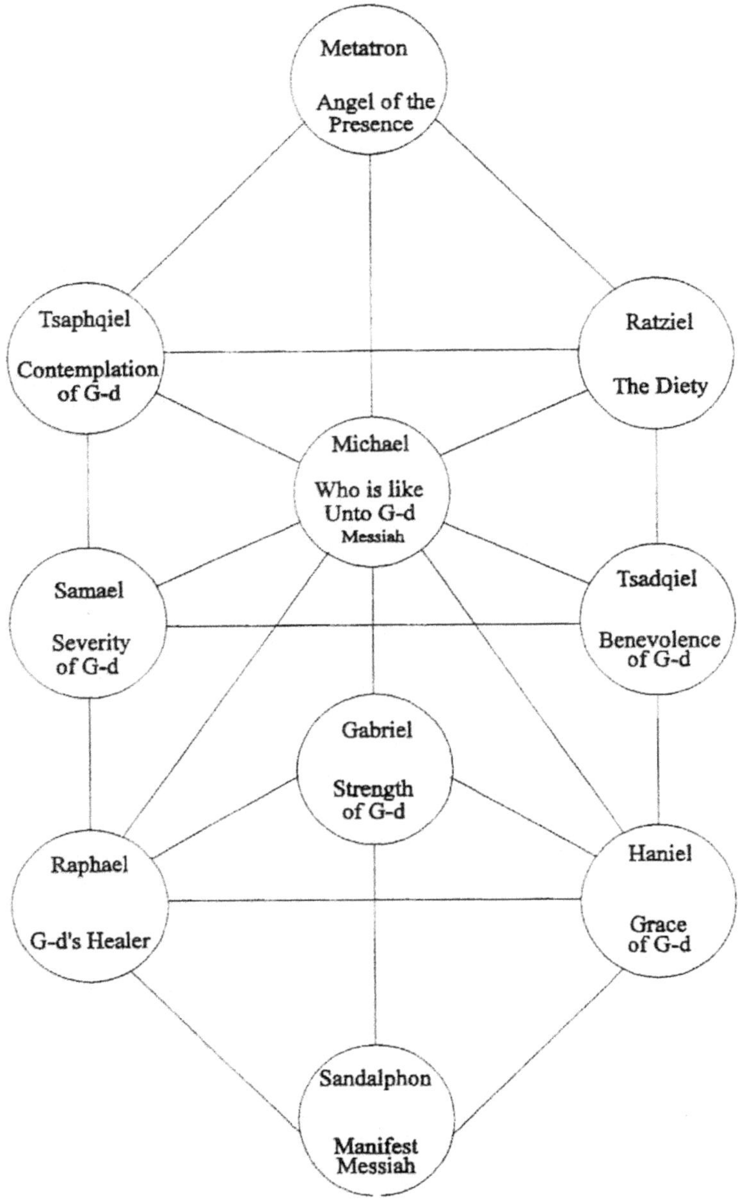

Contrary to popular belief, Angels are not male, although most have masculine names. The Zohar informs us that, when an Angel procures blessings for the world, he is male, but when called upon to chastise the world, the Angel is female (being as it were pregnant with judgment). As Angels are purely spiritual beings, they have neither a body nor, for that matter, a sex.

In picturing a heavenly body, man, in his ignorance, portrays Angels as being in the likeness of Man, performing their G-d given tasks the way Man does. An example of this is found in an ivory carving of an Angel discovered in Samaria dating to King Ahab, who lived in the ninth century BCE. This Angel has a human head, long hair and a lion-like body, with outstretched wings. In all probability, the artist was inspired by Babylonian art, and carved the figure in a similar style. The animal body with a human head seems to have been traditional, until, in the middle ages, European Jews used Angels with entirely human form to decorate their Passover Haggadoth, the books from which the Passover Service is recited. Fortunately this misleading practice stopped there.

The number and variations of man's portrayal of Angels in art are too numerous to count. So too, is it impossible to count the exact number of Angels, although many have tried to do so. Rabbi Simeon Ben Lakish, who lived in the third century CE, arrived at a figure, simply by computing the fact that, under each of the twelve signs of the zodiac, were thirty hosts of Angels. Now each host comprised thirty camps. Assembled under each camp were thirty legions of thirty cohorts. A cohort had thirty corps each consisting of 365,000 myriad. Therefore, taking each myriad as ten thousand Angels, the number of the Almighty's messengers was arrived at. Using Gematria as their basis, fourteenth century CE Kabalists arrived at a far more modest figure of a mere 301,655,722 Angels.

Metatron – Chaioth Ha Qodesh

Classified under the first Sephira - Keter or Crown - is the Angelic order of Chaioth Ha Qodesh (i.e. Holy Creatures), headed by the Archangel Metatron, the chief of chieftains, who is charged with the sustenance of mankind. The etymology of Metatron is disputed, but there is little doubt that the word is derived from Metator which means Messenger, Outrider, or Way-Maker.

As for the Chaioth Ha Qodesh, these holy living creatures are believed to be the same as those who appeared in the vision of *Ezekiel 9:2* :

> And, behold, six men came from the higher gate,
> which lieth toward the north, every man with his
> weapon of destruction in his hand: and one man
> in the midst of them clothed in linen, with a
> writer's ink-horn on his side....

Although they appeared as human beings to the prophet Ezekiel, the six men were powers of destruction in the form of Chaioth Ha Qodesh, charged with carrying out G-d's sentence. The seventh man, clothed in linen garments, and carrying writing implements at his side was, according to tradition, the Archangel Gabriel who placed on the foreheads of the righteous a "mark" - the letter Tav ת - in ink. The ink inscription denoted the word Tichyeh, meaning thou shalt live. On the brows of the wicked, Gabriel inscribed the same letter. This time, however, the initial was written in blood, and denoted the word Tamuth - thou shalt die.

The six executioners were ordered to follow the seventh man and slay without mercy all who bore no protective mark. It is interesting to note that these Angels did not have Metatron as their leader, but instead followed Gabriel who rules the Angelic order of Cherubim. The reason for this was because Gabriel, being the Strength of G-d, required greater powers of destruction than the more gentle Cherubim.

An Angel of the Chaioth Ha Qodesh - very likely Metatron himself - appears in a detailed, though highly controversial, description of the rebuilding of the Temple, prophesied to take place after the overthrow of Gog in the Messianic Age (*Ezekiel 40 - 48*).

The Angel is noted as having the appearance of Brass. The prophet Ezekiel discovers the Archangel measuring the outer and inner courts and buildings of the Temple. Metatron acts as Ezekiel's guide around the new temple, and informs him that the reason for Ezekiel being there is to report back to the people, in detail, all that he sees and thus strengthen the hope in their Final Deliverance.

Daniel 10:5-6 gives yet another vivid description of a Chaya Ha Qodesh:

> A man clothed in linen whose Loins were girded
> with the fine gold of Uphaz; his body was like
> beryl, and his face as the appearance of lightning
> and his eyes as torches of fire, and his arms and
> feet like in color to burnished brass, and the voice
> like the voice of a multitude.

This particular Angel is the one that promised Daniel a revelation of what Israel's fate would be in the End of Days or the Messianic Era.

According to Gematria, Metatron and Shadai (a term used for G-d Almighty) have the letters in each name add up to 314. This would explain why Metatron is often known as Little Adonai (Little Lord or G-d). It is this Archangel who is said to have been the conductor of the Children of Israel through the wilderness and of whom G-d says, "My name is in him". Metatron is called the Prince of faces and ruler of Moses. His name signifies the Angel of the Presence.

Metatron is sometimes called Yahel which means "In going out and coming back I am the Lord". It is through this ultimate individual agency that the Will of the Absolute can be communicated. It is also for this reason that Yahel has a particular interest in mankind. He has the power to send down the Holy Shechina, (the Holy Presence) to aid those who desire to draw near to the Divine. In this role, Metatron transmits Kabala throughout all levels of planes, so that all who wish to receive Kabala need only attune and "welcome" it (welcome is one of the many meanings given to the word Kabala).

The Archangel Metatron is the garment of Shadai or the visible manifestation of G-d. He governs the visible world, preserving the unity, harmony and the revolution of all the spheres, planets and heavenly bodies. He is the captain of the myriad of Angelic Hosts and is regarded as the "Kol Elohim" (Divine Voice). He is called the Great Teacher, the Teacher of Teachers. It is for this reason that Enoch, who walked in close communion with G-d, and taught mankind by his example, is said to have received the name Metatron, the Great Teacher, after he was taken into heaven (*Genesis* 5:24). Moreover, Metatron is the Angel of the Presence, the Angel of the Lord that was sent to go before the Children of Israel during their wanderings in the wilderness (*Exodus* 23:20-22):

> Behold I send an Angel before thee in the way, and
> to bring thee into the place which I have prepared.
> Beware of him, and obey his voice, provoke him not:
> for he will not pardon your transgressions: for My
> name is in him. But if thou shall indeed obey his
> voice, and do all that I speak: then I will be an
> enemy to thine enemies, and an adversary
> to thine adversaries.

The Almighty knew that the children of Israel would sin by building and worshipping the golden calf so He told Moses that He would no longer personally lead them with His Shechina, but would instead send the Archangel Metatron. Moses is warned in this passage that the people should not rebel against the Archangel because Metatron was not empowered to forgive the people's sins as would the Almighty who was long suffering and all merciful.

Knowing full well that as long as the Holy One was dwelling and moving within the midst of Israel, there was a perfect union between the Spirit [of G-d] and the spirit [of the people] so he, Moses, protested saying that unless the Almighty would continue to lead them, he and the Children of Israel would not continue their epic journey. [*"If thy presence go not, carry us not up hence" Exodus 33:15*] The Almighty conceded and told Moses that as long as Moses lived, He would continue to personally lead the Children of Israel. Later Metatron was sent to assist Joshua in leading the people in the conquest of the Holy Land. Joshua gratefully accepted the Angel because Joshua's spirituality was far lower than that of Moses the Law Giver.

While Moses was still in the cloud on Mt Sinai, he was met by the Angel Kamuel of whom it is said is the leader of twelve thousand other Angels of Destruction. Kamuel tried to overcome Moses and prevent him from receiving the Torah, but Moses spoke the twelve Names of G-d that were given to him at the burning bush and Kamuel immediately left him and kept himself at a great distance. Then another Angel, Hadraniel, whose name means the majesty of G-d, approached Moses. Moses was so terrified that he remained speechless until the Almighty reminded the law giver that he was not afraid of the Almighty at the burning bush, so why should he be terrified of a mere Angel and a good one at that! Moses then uttered the seventy two lettered name of G-d and the Angel Hadraniel befriended Moses and led him to the Archangel Sandalphon the brother of Metatron.

So exalted is Metatron's position in Ancient Jewish Angelology that we are told that when Elishah ben Abaja (also called Asher and said to be the fourth of the sages to enter Paradise) saw this Angel occupying the first position after the Almighty, he exclaimed "Peradventure, but far be it, there are two Supreme Powers". (*Talmud Chagiga 15a.*)

Abraham's servant (*Genesis 24:2*), according to the *Zohar (Vayesheb 181b)*, was Metatron and not Eliezer, as is popularly believed. Metatron was asked to put his hand under Abraham's thigh, as was the custom of the day when taking an important oath.

Since Metatron was in charge of restoring all the souls to their original bodies, this action may furthermore be interpreted as symbolizing the foundation of the world. Metatron was further charged not to choose Isaac's wife from among the daughters of the Canaanites, symbolizing that he should not take for a soul mate any of the maidens from the idolatrous nations. The Zohar further states that Metatron later takes ten camels, representing the Ten Sephirot over which he is said to exercise dominion.

The Angel of G-d mentioned in *Exodus 14:19-21*, is again said to be Metatron. One should note that each of these three verses contains seventy two letters. When each verse is written at length (in Hebrew) one above the other - the first from right to left, the second (starting from the bottom) from left to right, and the third (starting from the top) from right to left - they will render seventy two columns, or words, of three letters each. Each of the seventy two new words thus formed will be an attribute or name of the Deity. This is called the Shem Hamephorash or the divided name. Should the letters AL IH EL OR YAH be added to each of the triliteral names, one will obtain the names of seventy two Angels (see tables iv and v).

The following is a list of the names and functions of all seventy two Angels. These Angels are divided into nine groups of eight Angels each.

The first eight Angels mentioned are Seraphim who come under the aegis of Metatron:

1) **Vehuiah**: In the Kabala Vehuiah is considered as one of the eight Seraphim who are in charge of fulfilling prayers.

2) **Yeliel**: This Angel is known to be one of the guards of the gates of the South Wind. He also keeps harmony amongst married couples.

3) **Sitael**: A ruler of the nobility, Sitael helps when one feels overwhelmed by misfortune or is distressed.

4) **Elemiah**: In Sepher Yetzira, Elemiah is one of the 8 Seraphim guarding the Tree of Life. He also rules over voyages by sea and maritime expeditions.

5) **Mahasiah**: Mahasiah holds dominion over Science, philosophy and liberal arts as well as being one of the Angels of Peace.

6) **Lelahel**: Being an Angel of the Zodiac, this Angel is also the Guardian Angel of fortune, love, the sciences and the arts.

7) **Achaiah**: The name means "Trouble". In the Kabala Achaiah is not only one of the 8 Seraphim who guard the tree of life, he is also said to be the Angel of Patience and the Angel who discovered nature's secrets.

8) **Cahetel**: This agrarian Seraph is guardian over agricultural produce, and is in charge of increasing crop productivity.

The next eight Angels are of the order of the Cherubim whose leader is the Archangel Gabriel.

9) **Haziel**: As his name means "pity of G-d", Haziel dispenses G-d's pity, good faith and reconciliation.

10) **Aladia**: This Angel guards against rabies and the plague.

11) **Lauvia**: His name means G-d the Admirable, Lauviah's influence extends to sages and famous people.

12) **Hahaiah**: The Cherub Hahaiah, influences the thoughts of man and discloses the hidden mysteries of the Kabala.

13) **Yezalel**: Yezalel is the Guardian Angel of friendship, reconciliation and conjugal fidelity.

14) **Mebahel**: This Cherub has dominion over Justice, Truth and Liberty. He also protects innocence and reveals the truth.

15) **Hariel**: Hariel has control over tame beasts and guards against sinfulness. He also has dominion over the arts and sciences.

16) **Hakamiah**: comes to the assistance of those who wish to remove traitors from their midst. He also has influence over arms and arsenals. Hakamiah is now said to be the Guardian Angel of France.

The following 8 Angels are Aralim [Thrones] whose chief is Tsaphqiel.

17) **Leviah**: Leviah guards against sadness and insomnia. He influences wonderful discoveries and can bring revelations to the worthy while they sleep.

18) **Caliel**: A Throne Angel serving in the Second Heaven, Caliel controls the bringing of immediate assistance against hardship.

19) **Leuviah**: This Angel of the order of Aralim is the Angel of the Grace of G-d. He also brings man memory and intelligence.

20) **Pahaliah**: Pahaliah administers morals and theology. His name means G-d's redeemer.

21) **Nelchael**: He is also named the One and Only G-d and he rules over Mathematics, Geography and all the abstract sciences.

22) **Leiaiel**: Is an Angel presiding over the future, His name means the Right of G-d and it is he who awakens within us the awareness of inner and outer beauty.

23) **Melahel**: Melahel has dominion over plants that cure the sick. His name means "G-d who delivers us from sickness"

24) **Chahoel**: This Angel takes care of those in exile.

The fourth set of Angels is of the order of Chashmalim [Dominations] under the leadership of The Archangel Tsadqiel.

25) **Nith-haiah**: This Poet-Angel presides over the occult sciences and influences wise men who love peace and solitude.

26) **Haaiah**: Is the Angel who has dominion over diplomacy and ambassadors.

27) **Yerathel**: Yerathel dispenses the light of wisdom, and protects civilization and liberty.

28) **Seheiah**: A Chashmal who is in charge of protecting against fire, sickness and also governs longevity.

29) **Reiyel**: This Angel has dominion over religious sentiments, divine philosophy and meditation.

30) **Omael**: Omael multiplies species, perpetuates races and influences chemists.

31) **Lecabel**: Lecabel has dominance over all forms of agriculture and vegetation.

32) **Vasariah**: He is also known as "G-d is Just" and he is therefore the Angel of Justice and has dominion over judges, magistrates and lawyers.

Although the fifth set of Angels are of the order of "Seraphim," and as such should be led by Samael, they actually come under the sub-leadership of the Angel Camael. Camael's name means "He who sees G-d." and therefore it personifies Divine Justice which is more merciful than the severity of Samael.

33) **Iehuiah**: Iehuiah's name means "G-d who understands all things." It is for this very reason that this Angel is in charge of Divine Justice.

34) **Lehachia**: Known as "Merciful G-d," he is the embodiment of Peace and keeps subjects loyal to their ruler.

35) **Chavakiah**: "The Joy of G-d," Chavakiah has dominion over wills and testaments and keeps peace and harmony between family members.

36) **Menadel**: "G-d the Adorable," Menadel has control in repatriating exiles and freeing prisoners who have faith in the Lord Almighty.

37) **Aniel**: His name literally means "I am G-d." Aniel is not only one of the many guards of the West wind, he also inspires the sages in their meditations.

38) **Haamiah**: The protector of all who seek the truth, Haamiah is the guardian Angel of all monotheistic religions and helps man find the one true G-d.

39) **Rehael**: Rehael has dominion over health and longevity. He also is the upholder of the Fifth Commandment: "Honor thy father and thy mother."

40) **Ieiazel**: The "Rejoicer of G-d," Ieiazel is the Guardian Angel of books and libraries. He also brings solace to prisoners.

Next are the sixth group of Angels who are of the Order of the Bnei Elohim under the leadership of Raphael.

41) **Hahahel**: Hahahael is the guardian Angel of the pious.

42) **Mikael**: Not to be confused with the Archangel Michael, Mikael teaches us our responsibilities towards our duties to G-d and is the protector of those who go on long voyages.

43) **Veualiah**: Veualiah has dominance over the destruction of the enemy and he is also the deliverer from slavery.

44) **Ielahia**: Ielahiah is the protector of magistrates and also brings success in useful enterprises.

45) **Sealiah**: The confounder of those who have evil intentions, Sealiah also lifts up the humble and the crestfallen.

46) **Ariel**: His name means 'The Lion of G-d." Ariel is in charge of helping man discover all the beauty and bounty of the world. He also assists The Archangel Raphael in curing the sick.

47) **Asaliah**: Asaliah has dominion over Justice. He is also known as the Just Angel who reveals the Truth during court procedures. He also elevates the spirit of those who contemplate the Devine.

48) **Miahel**: Miahel is the Angel who brings love and fidelity and keeps the peace between those who are united in marriage.

The Tarshishim or Elohim form the seventh group of Angels, whose leader is Haniel.

49) **Vehuel**: Vehuel has dominance over those who show talent and virtue. He protects those who pay homage, bless, glorify and admire the Almighty.

50) **Daniel**: His name means "G-d is my Judge" and thus is the Guardian Angel of Justice, influencing lawyers and magistrates. He is also one of the Angels of Mercy.

51) **Hachashiah**: Some mistakenly say his name is Hachashel but Ambelain in his "La Kabbale Practique" quotes Sefer Yetzira, the book of Formation, as stating that the fifty first Angel is Hachashiah who is the protector of divine knowledge.

52) **Imamiah**: Imamiah has dominion over the destruction and humiliation of enemies. Strangely his name means the Quencher of G-d presumably because it is believed that the Almighty is satisfied when the wicked are taught a lesson and repent.

53) **Nanael**: This Scientific Angel also exercises his influence over teachers and those who uphold the law.

54) **Nithael**: Nithael has control over those who seek G-d's Mercy and those who deserve longevity.

55) **Mebahiah**: His Dominion is over morals and religion. He also assists those who are having difficulty in having children.

56) **Poiel**: Poiel has dominion over the renowned and also over fortune and philosophy.

The 8th group of Angels are the Malachim whose prince is Michael.

57) **Nemamiah**: Nemamiah is the Guardian Angel of just causes. He protects all aspects of the military when their fight is just.

58) **Yeialel**: Yeialel heals the broken hearted and also the maladies of the eyes.

59) **Herachel**: Herachel serves to prevent sterility in women and renders their children obedient and respectful towards their parents.

60) **Mitzrael**: Mitzrael serves to protect against persecution and cures those suffering from the afflictions of the spirit.

61) **Umabel**: His name means "Channel of G-d," for it is he who channels the Word of G-d to the correct quarters. He also has control over astronomy and physics.

62) **Iahahel**: Iahahel has dominion over those who wish to acquire wisdom, philosophers, the enlightened, and those who have withdrawn from mundane matters.

63) **Annauel**: Annauel helps protect against accidents heals the sick and dominates those who are in commerce.

64) **Mechiel**: Mechiel has dominion over sages and scholars. He protects against the rage of fierce animals and also brings the quintessence of being to all who seek it.

The Cherubim under Gabriel are the last group of Angels who bear the sacred names of the Shem Hamephorash.

65) **Damabiah**: Damabiah's dominion is over the seas, the rivers and their sources.

66) **Manakel**: Manakel is the authority over vegetation and aquatic animals. He also serves to appease the Wrath of G-d.

67) **Eiael**: Eiaiel makes known the truth in the Kabala and brings longevity to its seekers.

68) **Chabuiah**: Chabuiah has dominion over good health and cures the ill. He is also the guardian of agriculture and oversees the production of high-yielding crops.

69) **Rohel**: Rohel is set over the rich and famous. He is also responsible for revealing the whereabouts of stolen objects and brings to justice those who are responsible.

70) **Iabamiah**: Iabamiah controls all the generations of the animal kingdom as well as the phenomena of nature.

71) **Haiaiel**: Haiaiel is one of the Guardian Angels of Justice.

72) **Mumiah**: Mumiah has dominion over the sciences of chemistry, physics and medicine and brings health and longevity.

Many occultists who call themselves "Kabalists" have created a whole cult around these Angels and claim to have ways and means of invoking any or all of the above seventy two Angels to do their selfish, personal bidding. They often charge money to trusting people for this worthless information assuring them that their love lives or financial positions will improve. The gullible will believe that the occultists, through these particular Angels, do indeed have the power to change their lives but soon find disappointment. It is for this reason the ancient Rabbis or Masters strictly forbade such practices. A word of caution, Angels were created to serve the Almighty and will only do His bidding!

It is therefore futile and foolish for any one to believe that human beings have the power to summon an Angel in order to fulfill their selfish desire or commands. If one wishes to petition for anything, prayer and meditation and the power of positive thinking and moreover positive action are the only true channels to pursue.

TABLE IV

EXODUS 14 19-21

ויסע מלאך האלהים ההלך לפני מחנה ישראל וילך מאחריהם
ויסע עמוד הענן מפניהם ויעמד מאחריהם: ויבא בין
מחנה מצרים ובין מחנה ישראל ויהי הענן והחשך ויאר
את־הלילה ולא־קרב זה אל־זה כל הלילה: ויט משה
את־ידו על־הים ויולך יהוה את־הים ברוח קדים עזה
כל־הלילה וישם את־הים לחרבה ויבקעו המים:

19. *And the Angel of G-d, who went before them; removed and went behind them; and the pillar of cloud removed from before them, and stood behind them;*
20. *And it came between the camp of Egypt and the camp of Israel; and there was the cloud and the darkness here, yet gave it light by day there; and the one came not near the other all night.*
21. *And Moses stretched out his hand over the sea; and the Lord caused the sea to go back by a strong east wind all the night and made the sea dry land and the waters were divided*

18	17	16	15	14	13	12	11	10	9	8	7	6	5	4	3	2	1
ך	ל	ה	ה	ם	י	ה	ל	א	ה	ך	א	ל	מ	ע	ס	י	ו
ל	א	ק	ר	ב	ז	ה	א	ל	ז	ה	כ	ל	ה	ל	י	ל	ה
י	ו	ם	י	ה	ל	ע	ו	ד	י	ת	א	ה	ש	מ	ט	י	ו
36	35	34	33	32	31	30	29	28	27	26	25	24	23	22	21	20	19
ם	ך	ל	י	ו	ל	א	ר	ש	י	ה	נ	ח	מ	י	נ	פ	ל
ן	ו	ה	ח	ש	ך	ו	י	א	ר	א	ת	ה	ל	י	ל	ה	ו
ד	ק	ח	ו	ר	ב	ם	י	ה	ת	א	ה	ו	ה	י	ך	ל	ו
54	53	52	51	50	49	48	47	46	45	44	43	42	41	40	39	38	37
ן	נ	ע	ה	ד	ו	מ	ע	ע	ס	י	ו	ם	ה	י	ר	ח	א
י	ן	מ	ח	נ	ה	י	ש	ר	א	ל	ו	י	ה	י	ה	ע	נ
ת	א	ם	ש	י	ו	ה	ל	י	ל	ה	ל	כ	ה	ז	ע	ם	י
72	71	70	69	68	67	66	65	64	63	62	61	60	59	58	57	56	55
ם	ה	י	ר	ח	א	מ	ד	מ	ע	י	ו	ם	ה	י	נ	פ	מ
ו	י	ב	א	ב	י	ן	מ	ח	נ	ה	מ	צ	ר	י	ם	ו	ב
ם	י	מ	ה	ו	ע	ק	ב	י	ו	ה	ב	ר	ח	ל	ם	י	ה

TABLE V

THE SHEM HAMEPHORASH

In English characters

Note: the Hebrew letter Ayin is transcribed as O

18	17	16	15	14	13	12	11	10	9	8	7	6	5	4	3	2	1
K	L	H	H	M	I	H	L	A	H	K	A	L	M	O	S	I	V
L	A	Q	R	B	Z	H	A	L	Z	H	K	L	H	L	I	L	H
I	V	M	I	H	L	O	V	D	I	T	A	H	Sh	M	T	I	V
36	35	34	33	32	31	30	29	28	27	26	25	24	23	22	21	20	19
M	K	L	I	V	L	A	R	Sh	I	H	N	Ch	M	I	N	P	L
N	V	H	Ch	Sh	K	V	I	A	R	A	T	H	L	I	L	H	V
D	Q	Ch	V	R	B	M	I	H	T	A	H	V	H	I	K	L	V
54	53	52	51	50	49	48	47	46	45	44	43	42	41	40	39	38	37
N	N	O	H	D	V	M	O	O	S	I	V	M	H	I	R	Ch	A
I	N	M	Ch	N	H	I	Sh	R	A	L	V	I	H	I	H	O	N
T	A	M	Sh	I	V	H	L	I	L	H	L	K	H	Z	O	M	I
72	71	70	69	68	67	66	65	64	63	62	61	60	59	58	57	56	55
M	H	I	R	Ch	A	M	D	M	O	I	V	M	H	I	N	P	M
V	I	B	A	B	I	N	M	Ch	N	H	M	Tz	R	I	M	V	B
M	I	M	H	V	O	Q	B	I	V	H	B	R	Ch	L	M	I	H

If AL, El, or Yah is added to each of the above Triliteral names, the names of 72 Angels are obtained. These Angels rule over the 72 Quinaries of the degrees of the Zodiac.

Ratziel - Ophanim

Under the second Sephira, Chochmah or Wisdom, are classified the Ophanim - or wheels whose Archangel is Ratziel.

The Merkavah, Chariot, vision of *Ezekiel 1:1*, describes in absolute detail the appearance of these "chariot-like" Ophanim. It is widely agreed that Jewish mysticism, from its earliest beginnings down to the later studies of the Kabala centered on the vision of the Merkavah or Divine Throne-Chariot. It is also quite fitting that *Ezekiel 1:1-28* was chosen as the Haphtarah, the supplementary reading, usually taken from the prophets, for the first day of Shavuot, for it immediately follows the Torah reading recounting the Great Theophany, the appearance of the Almighty, on Mount Sinai.

The Prophet's vision actually contains two types of heavenly hosts - the Chaioth and the Ophanim. Each Chaya had four faces, representing the heads of four kingdoms. At the front was the face of a man (representing intelligent beings), while to the right appeared the face of a lion (kingdom of the beasts). The left face was that of an ox (domesticated animals), and the face at the rear was that of an eagle (representing the birds). When the Divine Throne Chariot departed however, the face of the ox was changed to that of a Cherub. This was because a Cherub was needed to guard the chariot on its way back from whence it came. Cherubs also guarded the entrance to the Garden of Eden after the expulsion of Adam and Eve. *(Genesis 3:24)* Another reason for the change was because the Chaioth of the Merkavah, or Divine Throne Chariot, were equated to the Cherubim and so, having performed their duty so admirably the 'ox face' was changed to that of a Cherub denoting that they were equitable.

> "And physiognomy does not consist in the
> external lineaments but in the features
> which are mysteriously drawn in us. The
> features in the face change according to
> the form which is peculiar to the inward
> face of the spirit. It is the spirit which
> produces all these facial peculiarities known
> to the wise; and it is only through the spirit
> that the features have any meaning. All
> these spirits and souls which proceed from
> Eden (i.e. the Highest Wisdom) have a
> peculiar form which is reflected in the face"...
> *(Zohar ii 736)*

"The face, thus lit up by the peculiar spirit inhabiting the body, is the mirror of the soul. The formation of the head indicates the character and temperament of each person. An arched forehead is a sign of a cheerful and profound spirit with distinguished intellect. A round but flat forehead indicates foolishness and silliness. A forehead that is flat and compressed on the sides and somewhat spiral in shape, shows vanity and a narrow mind." *(Zohar ii 716, 75a).*

The legs of each Chaya sparkled like burnished brass and were straight without joints. Since they did not have to turn around or lie down, they did not need joints. Their feet had soles, like a calf's, to enable them to make their way smoothly in each direction. Each had four wings. Under each wing they had the hand of a man. Two of their wings were spread above the face and were joined on both sides to their neighbor's wings, thus hiding each other's face. The other two wings covered the body of each of the Ophanim.

The Ophanim were not stationary, but galloped to and fro with the speed of lightning, guided all the time by the Divine Will.

One wheel (or Ophan), which was the color of beryl (very likely the color of a golden Topaz), was assigned to each Chaya. Each gigantic wheel was intersected at right angles, creating the effect of a wheel within a wheel. In their midst was lightning and radiance. Although the Ophanim had eyes and their own intelligence, they had no independent movement, and could only move with the Chaioth. Both moved as intended by the Divine Presence. (Note: some interpret the Divine Presence in the Merkavah to be the Shechina whilst others interpret it as being the Messiah. Both are equally correct.)

Ratziel is the Herald of the Deity. He is the Flash of Wisdom or the Secrets of G-d that are "sent forth". He is also known as the Angel of the secret regions and chief of the Supreme Mysteries. Other names that are given to him are Akrasiel, Suriel, and Saraqiel. Ratziel is said to spread his wings over the Chaioth, who uphold the universe so that their fiery breath does not consume the other ministering Angels.

Tradition states that Ratziel befriended Adam when he was evicted from the Garden of Eden. He gave Adam a book containing the wisdom of the Kabala. This book, known as *Sefer Ratziel* or the *Book of the Angel Ratziel*, came into the possession of Enoch, who is said to have obtained from it knowledge for his own book, *The Book of Enoch*. The *Sepher Ratziel* was later given, via Noah, to Abraham, who took it with him when he went to Egypt, where the patriarch allowed a portion of this mystical doctrine to be revealed. It was in this way that the Egyptians obtained some knowledge of it, and they introduced it to the other eastern nations, which in turn, made it part of their respective philosophical systems.

The book was passed from Abraham on to Isaac, then to Jacob, who gave it to Levi, whose descendant Moses - already very learned and initiated in all the wisdoms of Egypt received it. During his forty years in the wilderness, Moses became most proficient in the Kabala, devoting all his leisure hours to its study. According to Kabalistic tradition, Moses had as his teacher the Archangel Ratziel, who graciously communicated to him the heavenly doctrine. Moses would later share his knowledge with the children of Israel, and thereby enable the righteous to return to their pristine nobility and felicity. Moses passed on the tradition to the seventy elders of Israel (the Sanhedrin) who, in turn, passed it from hand to hand, until it came to King Solomon, who learned the Secrets of the Universe from it.

From the *Book of the Angel Ratziel* we also learn that there are seven Angels who stand before the Throne of the Lord. They are Gabriel, Fanuel, Michael, Uriel, Raphael, Israel, and Uzziel.

Tsaphqiel - Aralim

The third Sephira is known as Binah or Intelligence and to this feminine passive potency, is ascribed the Angelic order of Aralim, headed by their prince or chieftain, Tsaphqiel. The word Aralim means Thrones and some scholars claim that the Aralim are mentioned in *Isaiah 33:7*.

In his vision of the deliverance of Zion, Isaiah addresses himself to the Assyrians: "... behold their valiant ones (the Hebrew word is Erellam) cry without; their ambassadors of peace weep bitterly..." The Hebrew Erellam is sometimes rendered as "their valiant ones" (as above) while others translate the word to mean "G-d's Lions", or even "Inhabitants of Ariel". Still other sources claim that the prophet meant Aralim, which, in this particular context, and taking the preceding verse into account, would make sense. It is very interesting to note that this is the only reference to this order of Angels in the Old Testament.

The Aralim (sometimes spelt Erelim) are composed of white fire and number 70 000 myriad. They are in charge of grass, fruit, trees and grain.

As he comes under the influence of the Sephira, Binah, Tsaphqiel is the Archangel of Understanding, and is called Beholder of G-d as well as the Contemplation of G-d. It is also said that he rules the planet Saturn on the

Sabbath. He is associated with the "primal waters" of Understanding and is also known as the Prince of Spiritual Strife against evil.

Tsaphqiel is not only the receptive and formulative principle of the Universe, but is also the watcher over all that is below. As the restraining influence in observing the world, he has been called the All-Seeing Eye of G-d.

The All-Seeing Eye has always meant the all-pervading consciousness of G-d or His universal vision. No matter where man may go, or try to hide, he can never evade the Divine consciousness represented by the All-Seeing Eye because he is ever within the vision of the Divine system of laws.

This sign appears in many cultures during different eras. In ancient Egypt we find the Eye of Horus. Buddhists believe in the third eye, while many occult and mystical societies such as the Free Masons and the Rosicrucians have adapted it as one of their symbols. It appears on the great seal of the United States of America and on that country's one dollar bill. It is even used to ward off the Evil Eye where such beliefs in the power of the Evil Eye occur.

Mark Twain described it most succinctly: "The common eye sees only the outside of things, and judges by that, but the 'All -Seeing eye' pierces through, and reads the heart and the soul, finding there capacities which the outside didn't indicate or promise, and which the other kind couldn't detect."

It is so easy to dismiss the Evil Eye as an instrument of folklore where often the casting of the Evil Eye is unintentional especially when it is mainly caused by envy. In Southern Europe and the Middle East one wards off the Evil Eye simply by wearing a blue bead made of glass or turquoise, whereas in Eastern Europe a red woolen strand is worn on the wrist. But, according to the Kabala, one should not underestimate this serious need to confront the problem of negative influences. Some charlatans try to influence the gullible by making them wear a red woolen string for which they charge exorbitant prices. The only accepted way to ward off the Evil Eye is to hold positive thoughts and believe that the Evil Eye will have no negative effect upon us. Our consolation is in the knowledge that whoever casts the Evil Eye will in fact have that same evil revisit those that have cast the Evil Eye whether it was done wittingly or unwittingly.

Tsadqiel - Chashmalim

The union of the second and third Sephirot produced Chesed (Mercy) which is represented by the order of Chashmalim (Scintillating Flames) headed by the Archangel Tsadqiel.

The Chashmalim are also known as Dominations. In its singular form (Chashmal) the word is often translated as Electrum *(Ezekiel 1:4)*; but in the *Zohar,* the term denotes "an inner, supernal sphere, hidden and veiled, in which the mysteries of the celestial letters of the Holy Name are suspended *(Talmud Hagiga 13)*. To some, Chashmal was in fact an Angel who was of the order of Chaioth of the Speaking Fire. The Hagiga relates the tale that there was once a young man who was so wrapped in the study of the vision of Ezekiel, and contemplated the Angel Chashmal so intensely that the latter consumed him with fire. It is probably from this story that many Rabbis are led to believe that one should not study Kabala as a young man. They recommend that it is advisable to wait till one is married and at least 40 years of age.

As illustrated in Tables i, ii and iii, just below the Archangel Michael, on the two sides of the Ten Sephirot, are the Beriatic Gevurah (Judgment) and Chesed (Mercy). These are presided over by the Archangels Samael (Severity of G-d) and Tsadqiel (the Righteousness or Benevolence of G-d). It is interesting to note that Tsadqiel also means the Nobleness of G-d since Nobility lives with Righteousness. The two Archangels keep equilibrium, for, if Mercy were not checked by Judgment, creation would be in chaos. Any imbalance would result in either too much rigor, or excess power. The Archangel Michael reconciles the two forces under the conscious direction of the Divine Will.

Throughout the Kabala and the Bible, much is written about the Angel of Mercy, although his actual name, Tsadqiel is hardly ever mentioned. This is because Tsadqiel is the instrument responsible for carrying out the Almighty's infinite mercy, and as his agent, modestly adopts a low profile. The lesson here is that we too, like obedient servants, should go quietly about our Master's work, without demanding or shouting out for recognition or reward.

When Adam and Eve were expelled from Eden, the gentle Angel of Mercy, Tsadqiel, did not forsake them, but taught them repentance. In this way, Adam and Eve were paradoxically brought nearer to their Creator while outside of Eden than when they were in that garden of paradise.

When Balaam set out to curse the children of Israel *(Numbers 22:22)*, "The Angel of the Lord" - actually the Angel of Mercy - appeared first before Balaam's ass, and then to Balaam himself. In this way he restrained Balaam from committing a mortal sin and thus perishing.

Tsadqiel has been awarded the titles of the Angel of Mercy, the Angel of Memory, and the Angel of Benevolence. He is also one of the seven Archangels who stand in the Presence of the Almighty. Together with the Archangel Tsaphqiel, the Archangel of the Aralim, he is said to assist Michael when he raises his flag, or standard, in Holy Battle.

Tsadqiel was present when Abraham was about to sacrifice his only son, Isaac. Accompanied by the Archangel Michael, Tsadqiel held back the Patriarch's hand. It was while Tsadqiel held back Abraham's hand that Michael called out to Abraham to stop the sacrifice of his son, Isaac. Because Angels can only perform one task at a time, one again sees two tasks being executed by two separate Angels.

Tsadqiel is described as the Guardian Angel of Abraham as well as the Force of Intelligence, and the Angel of the planet Jupiter. In Rabbinic writings, he is also known as the Angel of benevolence, mercy, and memory.

Samael - Seraphim

The "Sword Clad" Seraphim, headed by Samael are placed within the fifth Sephira which is Gevurah (Judgment), also known as Pachad (Fear). Seraphim are the symbols of G-d's presence. It is for this reason that Cherubim, together with the flaming sword [symptomatic of the Seraphim], were appointed to guard the Garden of Eden after Adam and Eve's expulsion. *(Genesis 3:24.)*

When King Uzziah died, the Prophet Isaiah gave a clear description of the Seraphim:

> I saw the Lord sitting upon a throne high and
> lifted up, and his train filled the temple.
> Above Him stood the Seraphim each one
> had six wings with twain he covered his face,
> and with twain he covered his feet, and with
> twain he did fly. And one called unto
> another and said:
> Holy, Holy, Holy, the Lord of hosts.
> The whole earth is full of His Glory...
> *(Isaiah 6: 1-3)*

This passage is the only one in the Old Testament that mentions the Seraphim by name, it depicts each Seraph covering his face as a mark of reverence, since even ministering Angels dare not gaze upon the Divine Presence. Each covered his feet in modesty, so as not to expose all his body. In the Midrash, the soles of the Seraphim are described as that of a calf.

Since a calf is a reminder of when some of the Children of Israel worshipped the golden calf while Moses received the Ten Commandments, the Seraphim are here described as covering their feet so as not to recall that sin before the Almighty. The words, "Holy, Holy, Holy," known as the trisagion, are now also used in the liturgy of most Orthodox Christian sects. In Judaism they are repeated in the Amidah, a prayer recited at least thrice daily by all pious Jews. We see, then, that this vision was so important that it was introduced in its entirety into the liturgy of the daily prayer book, and is read in both Hebrew and Aramaic. The latter was the lingua franca spoken throughout the Middle East during the time of the second temple and is still retained in certain prayers to this day.

Following this momentous vision, the prophet Isaiah felt that his own spiritual shortcomings would be an insurmountable barrier between himself and the Divine Summons. To allay these fears, a Seraph flew down and with a glowing stone, taken from the altar, touched Isaiah's lips with it. As the fire on the altar was holy, it burned away his iniquities and expiated his sins. *(Isaiah 6:6-7)*.

The Seraphim have long been considered the highest order of Angels. Since time immemorial, the honor of being the Chieftain of the Seraphim was given to the Archangel Samael. This has been questioned by many, mainly non Jewish, writers and students.

Samael among his numerous roles was also given the unenviable position of Satan, which in Hebrew means the Accuser. To some of these writers and students, Satan is synonymous with the Devil who is erroneously and sadly given the label of a "Fallen Angel." According to them, a fallen Angel could not possibly head so illustrious an echelon of Angels as the Seraphim and so they were quick to appoint a new ruling prince.

In their haste they have not only selected one but several chieftains, namely: Seraphiel, Metatron, Michael and even Jehoel, who is traditionally the Angel who restrains the Leviathan and keeps it in check.

This confuses the issue even more, because the question now arises as to who is in fact the correct leader. The answer is simple if one accepts the fact that Samael is definitely not a fallen angel but has always been the Archangel and Prince of the Seraphim. Samael is the Severity of G-d and as such, he upholds the Sefirah of Strength or Judgment, Gevurah [see table i].

It must be remembered that if Judgment is not tempered by Mercy through Compassion, it lashes out and destroys life. Here lies the origin of evil and is probably the reason that Samael is wrongly considered to be 'evil.'

The Archangel of the Seraphim, Samael, also assumes the role of the Angel of Death. He is often called Khamael, the burner of G-d. In both these roles, he carries out the task of eliminating imperfections in creation. The etymology of the word Sami is blind, and Samael is sometimes known as the Guardian Angel of the Blind. In Gematria, his name numerically equals Ophan, which means Throne. This shows that this Angel is, in fact, a good Angel, branded with a bad reputation because of the fact that he was given, as his main duty, the task of tempting man, and then accusing him should he succumb to the temptation. It is for this reason that he is also called The Accuser or Satan.

Solomon in his wisdom wrote in *Proverbs 16:14*: "The wrath of a king is as Angels of death: but a wise man will pacify it." This wise saying has a double meaning. Not only will the wise man pacify the wrath of his king but he will control his actions by not allowing himself to be tempted into doing foolish things that he might later regret.

Samael also holds sway over Demons, who constitute the lower class of Angels, inhabiting the Assiatic world (Olam Assiah-the world of action). They are the grossest and most deficient of all forms, the Klippot (shells or husks) of Being. According to the Sephirot, they too form ten degrees, but here darkness and impurity increase with the descent of each degree.

The first two degrees are nothing more than the absence of all visible form and organization, which in Genesis is described as 'Tohu va Vohu' – 'without form and void.' The third degree is the abode of darkness which the book of Genesis describes as having, in the beginning, "covered the face of the deep". Next follow seven infernal halls or hells, occupied by the demons which are the incarnation of all human vices. They are the ones who torture those poor, deluded beings, who allow themselves to be led astray on this earthly plane. These seven infernal halls are subdivided into endless compartments which act as separate chambers of torture for every type of sin.

In the Bible, *1 Chronicles 21:1* the prince of this region is called Satan (which means "Adversary"), and in the Kabala, Samael, Angel of Poison or Death). He is the same spirit that seduced Eve. His wife, or female counterpart, is called Lillith, the Harlot, or the woman of whoredom, but they are generally represented as united in the one name of the Beast, the snake. There is a legend where Lillith is said to have been Adam's first wife. She was so evil that Adam left her and was given Eve.

Rabbi Simeon is quoted in the Zohar as stating that Samael came down from Heaven, riding on a serpent to seduce Eve. Samael imbued the snake with his spirit, so that whatever the snake spoke to Eve, was actually inspired by this Archangel.

Thus, he brought death and curses into the world, and through Wisdom, destroyed the first tree that G-d had created:

> This responsibility rested on Samael until another holy tree came, namely Jacob, who wrested the blessing from him (*Genesis 32: 24*), in order that Samael might not be blessed above and Esau below. Jacob was the reproduction of Adam and he had the same spiritual beauty as Adam. Just as Samael withheld blessings from the first tree, so Jacob, who was the same tree as Adam, withheld blessings from Samael; in doing so Jacob but took back his own". *(Zohar Bereshith 35b.)*

The Zohar *(Vayishlah 170a)* is quite clear that the man (*Genesis 32:24*) who wrestled with Jacob was none other than Samael, the chieftain of Esau. As the angel realised that Jacob was gaining the upper hand, he wounded Jacob's thigh, leaving him with a limp. As a reminder of that struggle, and to defy the Adversary, the sciatic nerve and arteries and tendons must first be removed, before the thigh of a ritually slaughtered animal is declared fit for consumption (Kosher) by the descendants of Jacob. Jacob continued wrestling with Samael, who realised that the dawn would break, and with it his power would decrease and vanish. This was because the Archangel was also needed for the early morning choir which sang praises to the Almighty, he then begged Jacob to let him go. Jacob held on until daybreak, when he was blessed and his name changed to Israel. There are three meanings attributed by the Rabbis to this sacred name: Champion of G-d; Prince-hood and Strength; and he who wrestled with the Angel.

The idea of the Serpent which seduced Eve is not particular to the Kabala. It is stated in the *Talmud, Baba Bathra, 16a:*

> The evil spirit, Satan, and the Angel of Death
> are the same. It is propounded in the Boraith
> that he descends and seduces; he then
> ascends and accuses and then comes down
> again and kills.

The Bahir *200* gives us the reason why Samael seduced Eve. It relates that on hearing that the Almighty had given man dominion of the fowl of the air (*Genesis 1:26*) Samael mistook this to included all the flying things of the heaven which also incorporated Angels. He therefore made a pact with the entire host on high and decided to make Adam sin and be exiled from before the Almighty. He cunningly chose Eve and, according to what followed, had intercourse with her.

The Talmud *(Baba Bathra, fol. 17)* tells us that the Angel of Death had no power over the following six people, of whom it is written that the Shechina took their souls with a kiss:

Abraham, Isaac, Jacob, Moses, Aaron, and Miriam.

In the Talmud *(Abodah Zarah, 20)* Samael, in his role as the Angel of Death, is described as being "Altogether full of eyes". At the time of the death of a terminally ill person, Samael takes his place above the invalid's head. In the Angel's hand is a drawn sword, with a drop of poison suspended on it and at the appointed time he lets the fatal dose fall into the invalid's mouth.

According to the *Zohar 9b*, when Cain was banished from the earth, he descended into Arka, one of the seven nether worlds. There he met up with Aftira and Kastimon, the two chiefs of that world. Prior to Cain's arrival, the chiefs were at perpetual war with each other. They bore the likeness of holy Angels, having six wings, though one had the face of an ox, and the other that of an eagle. When Cain forced them to make peace, they joined together as one body, and assumed the physical likeness and spiritual image of Man. In times of darkness these creatures change into the form of a two-headed serpent and reach the abode of Uzza and Azael, the descendants of Cain. They are greatly stirred and aroused, believing that the Day of Judgment has arrived. From there, the creature tries to approach Na'amah (also known as Lillith), the mother of the demons, who first seduced Adam and Eve. Na'amah then assumes all shapes and forms in order to lead astray the sons of man, while the two chiefs return to their abode where they, in turn, arouse the sensual desires in the descendants of Cain to bear children.

There are many of the opinion that once we have all achieved perfection on earth, the restitution of all things will take place. Satan will be restored as the Angel of Light, because he too, like all other beings, came from the same Source of all things. The first part of his name will then be dropped, and he will retain the second part -EL- which is the common name of all Archangels. This, however, will only take place at the coming of the Messiah, when hell will disappear and all souls will return to the bosom of G-d, from whence they came.

We are told in a later Aggada that Samael does not know the path to the Tree of Life, but flies to and fro in search of it. Samael has one long hair that grows out of his navel. While the hair is intact, his reign continues. However, with the coming of the Messiah, the hair will break off at the sound of the Great Shofar and Samael will have fulfilled his purpose and no longer have the need to accuse Man.

Several references to Samael are made in various versions of the flood story. When Noah was shown the rainbow for the first time, the Almighty told him that whenever Satan would accuse and condemn mankind at a critical time, demanding that the rain should be turned into a deluge to bring destruction to the world, the Lord would then consider the rainbow and remember his covenant never to destroy the world by flood again.

This is why a rainbow appears after the rain to remind us that even though we may be wicked, the Almighty will never again destroy the world by flood, but we should nevertheless mend our ways.

The Midrash tells of an interesting story of how Noah, the father of the plough, took some vine cuttings with him into the ark. Once the flood had subsided and the earth was ready to be planted, instead of sowing wheat or grain - crops vital to the survival of mankind - Noah planted a vineyard.

As Noah was about to plant his first vine, Satan appeared before him and asked to be made a partner in the produce of the vineyard. Noah agreed and watched while Satan first slaughtered a little lamb over the vine. Next a Lion was killed, and the vine was saturated with its blood. Then followed the killing of a monkey, whose blood was also spilled over the vine. Lastly, the blood of a pig was poured over the earth under the vine. For this reason, excessive drinking leads to satanic consequences. If a man has one cup of wine, he becomes docile and peaceful like a lamb. After his second cup, he becomes like a lion, and boasts of the things he believes he will accomplish. His third cup leads him to dance and act like a monkey. After his fourth cup, he vomits and rolls in the mud like a pig.

Many have the misguided idea that Satan is a "Fallen Angel." The idea of Fallen Angels is not found anywhere in the Old Testament for it is not a Jewish concept at all. The notion is often expressed in post-biblical literature that has been influenced by paganism whose concepts have exerted an acute belief in the existence of the forces of Good against the powers of Evil. Even the Nephilim (giants) in *Genesis 6:4* are erroneously referred to as Fallen Angels but Maimonides quashed that idea by explaining that the Nephilim were the sons of rulers and judges.

Too much emphasis is placed on the fact that Samael is the Angel of Death and Satan. Some scholars go as far as saying that on Yom Kippur he accuses Israel and calls for the annihilation of the Jews. This is refuted by a strong majority who believe that Satan, in Hebrew, has the numerical value of 364. And for 364 days he persists on accusing Israel of going astray and being unworthy of the title of "The Chosen People". But on the 365th day of the year - Yom Kippur - he takes back his accusations and admires Israel for their prayers of praise and their atonement, or rather "at - onement," with the Almighty.

It is true that he is the "Poison of G-d", but only as the evil tempter. Man is a free agent. If one does not succumb, but rises above temptation, Samael is powerless to act as the accuser, and eventually as the Angel of Death. Hell is what one makes of one's life on earth. Righteousness the love of one's fellow man, and the study of the Torah, will turn that hell into Heaven right here on earth.

The Zohar *(Vayigash 209a)* explains it very clearly:

> Observe that if a man is jealous for the Holy One;
> Blessed be He, the Angel of Death has no Power
> over him as he has over other men, and to him
> is given the covenant of peace...

Michael Malachim

The sixth Sephira, Tipheret or Beauty, has Michael as Champion of the Malachim. The word Malachim is translated as Angels or kings. This order of Angels is equated with the order of Virtues, one of which is the Angel Ariel (Lion of G-d). Michael means, "Who is like unto G-d" or "Messiah", and, as such, is traditionally attributed as being the Guardian Angel of the Jews. He is too often depicted as contending with the dragon of Satan in a heavenly cosmic war between the hosts of order and those of disorder. It must be understood that Satan does not own dragons except in mythology. Being the central pivot of the Beriatic world, and Tiferet (Beauty) of the Yetziratic world, he is the obvious choice as the Guardian of Heaven and the Watcher of Man. Michael is invested with Divine Protection and Sovereign Power, and rests at the foot of the Throne that rides the Chariot of Ezekiel's vision.

"But the Prince of Persia withstood me..." (*Daniel 10:13*) is the first time that the Bible gives a clear reference to the fact that each Nation has its own Guardian Angel. Although not definitely stated, this belief is presupposed thus showing that the author is dealing with a conviction already familiar to its readers.

From the foregoing verse there is no doubt whatsoever that the Patron Angel of Israel is Michael. This is again asserted in *Daniel 10:21*, with the words, "Michael your Prince." We see it yet again in *Daniel 12:1* where it is proclaimed that the

Archangel Michael will deliver Israel, and thus herald in the Messianic Age, which will inaugurate the Era of Eternal Bliss.

The Zohar *(Bereshith 143a)* in its justification of Isaac's decision to bless Jacob instead of Esau states that when Isaac spoke to Esau, he uttered the words, "That I may bless thee Before the Lord" *(Genesis 27:4)*. At that moment, the Throne of the Almighty shook and trembled, saying, "Will the serpent now be released from its curses and Jacob become subject to them?"

The Archangel Michael, accompanied by the Shechina, immediately appeared before Jacob. The aged, yet highly enlightened, Isaac sensed this, and blessed his younger son, Jacob, in the presence of Michael. From that time on, Michael became the protector of Jacob and his descendants, the people of Israel.

The Aggada states that both Michael and Gabriel are consistently identified as the many anonymous divine messengers mentioned in the Bible. We thus identify Michael as being one of the three Angels who visited Abraham after his circumcision *(Genesis 18:2)*. It was his duty to inform the patriarch that his wife Sarah would soon have a male child. As already mentioned, it was Michael who called out to Abraham not to offer up his son Isaac as a sacrifice *(Genesis 22:11)*.

Some scholars say that the reason why the Angel called Abraham's name twice was to show anxiety in holding Abraham back, even to the very last moment. Others give the more plausible reason that there appears in the original text a disjunctive mark between the two Abraham's, in order to show that the new Abraham was not at all like the former. The first Abraham was still incomplete, whereas the second Abraham refers to the perfected Abraham who, in his complete obedience, had not withheld his only son before the Lord.

According to the Aggada, when Abraham refused to acknowledge King Nimrod as a god, the king cast Abraham into the fiery furnace. Michael rescued Abraham by cooling down the flames and causing blossoms to appear on the wood. As a result Abraham was released. Later Michael informed Abraham of Lot's capture and assisted in the destruction of all the Kings that had captured Lot. Michael accompanied Abraham's servant, Eliezer (who is also identified as the Archangel Metatron), on his quest to find a wife for Isaac.

Together with Gabriel, Michael was called upon to record that Esau had sold his birthright to Jacob. This "birthright" is often misrepresented as a physical inheritance of worldly goods, which is not the case at all. When he fled Esau's wrath Jacob left behind his entire father's earthly possessions to his elder brother as was the custom of the time. Jacob took only a spiritual birthright, and thus became the inheritor and custodian of the knowledge that was taught by Abraham and Isaac, which he later passed on to the tribes of Israel.

One of the many legends attributed to Michael is when on the day that King Solomon married the daughter of Pharaoh Neco, Michael came down to earth and stuck a reed in the sea, around the reed some matter settled. Upon this earthly matter, the future destroyer of Israel, Rome, was built.

Second Kings 19:35 tells us of the sudden annihilation of Sennacherib's army, composed of 5,180 men. This was attributed to the Archangel Michael. He also acted as defender of the Jews against every charge that Haman brought against them (*Esther* 3:6). The Archangel was even instrumental in thrusting Haman up against Queen Esther, to make it appear as though Haman wished to violate his queen. It is said that Michael is composed entirely of snow, while Gabriel is made of fire. These two Archangels do not injure each other, although they both stand near another. They illustrate the power of the Almighty in bringing two opposite forces together and thus they "Make Peace in His High Places".

Haniel - Elohim (Tarshishim)

The mystical seventh Sephira, Netzach, is Firmness and Victory. It is here that the Angelic Hosts, Elohim or Tarshishim (the brilliant ones), are headed by the Archangel Haniel. Elohim is the common name given to G-d. In *1 Samuel 28:13*, the woman of Endor informs Saul that she saw "gods ascending out of the earth". The term gods is rendered from the word "Elohim", which could be a reference to these Angelic hosts. The woman in fact saw Samuel but because he was a spirit she called him "gods or G-d-Like". Tarshish is Hebrew for pearl, hence the Tarshishim are called the Brilliant Ones, or Angels of Virtue.

Haniel is often called "The Glory of the Grace of G-d, or he who sees G-d". He is said to have been closely associated with Enoch and was thus given the task of transporting Enoch to heaven (*Genesis 5:24*). Haniel seems to have many variants to his name, including Hamiel, Hanael, Onoel and Anael. Most of these names are steeped in legend. For example Onoel is said to be one of the seven Archons (Archons are Angels who guard nations). In some circles he is cited as being a hostile demon who takes on the form of an ass.

Haniel is mentioned twice in the Bible, but not as an Angel. In *1 Chronicles 7:39*, Haniel is an Asherite, the son of Ulla, and a mighty man of valor. In *Numbers 34:23*, he is a Prince of Manasseh, the son of Ephod, who represented his tribe in the division of Canaan.

As he is in charge of the virtuous or righteous, it is the Archangel Haniel who proclaims "Open ye the gates that the righteous nation that keepeth faithfulness may enter in" *(Isaiah 26:2)*. Here Isaiah is quoting the Archangel Haniel. A beautiful Rabbinical interpretation of this phrase is that the righteous of all nations shall have a share in the World to Come.

Haniel is said to be the Chief of Principalities, and the "tallest Angel in Heaven". The role of the principalities, the third group in the hierarchy of Angels, is said to be the care takers of all nations on earth. As such they directly influence all the affairs of humanity and have the capability of changing the hearts and minds of a whole nation for the amelioration of mankind. We are told that Haniel is also in charge of the planet Capricorn and its ruling astrological sign.

Unfortunately very little else is written about Haniel. Most of his attributes and actions were never written down and were only passed down orally and have therefore, sadly been lost over time.

Raphael - Bnei Elohim

The Angels, Bnei Elohim, (Children of G-d), bring up the eighth Sephira, Hod (Splendor). The Archangel Raphael heads these Angels, who, some say, are first mentioned in *Genesis 6:4*. Many Rabbis argue that the words "Bnei Ha Elohim" should in this instance, be interpreted to mean "sons of the mighty", and not "sons of G-d", as is commonly suggested in most Bibles. Since it is absolutely foreign to Jewish thought that Angels should marry humans, the passage is seen as depicting the sons of nobles, or the powerful, who took as their wives the daughters of the people, too powerless to resist. These marriages were the result of unbridled passion, and indicative of the oppression and evil ways of that period. Yet another explanation of the Bnei Ha Elohim is that they were those who believed in the Almighty and, as such, were entitled to the name "sons of G-d". It was only when they intermarried with the "daughters of man" (idolaters) that they became ungodly.

According to the Midrash, however, the Bnei Ha Elohim were in fact, the sons of Angels. We are told in the Midrash *(Bereshith)* that when the Lord deplored the wickedness of man, the Angels Shamhazael and Azael reminded Him that they were the ones who had warned him of the unworthiness of Man to become one of G-d's creations, and that Man should never have been created at all. The Lord replied that if it were not for Man, the universe would serve no purpose. Shamhazael and Azael argued that the Angels were sufficient reason for the existence of the universe, and implored G-d to send them down to earth so that they could prove that they would sanctify the Lord's name, and not possess evil as men did. Hence, Shamhazael and Azael were sent down to live on earth as two human beings. However, when they experienced the beauty of human women, they could not resist the temptation to sin with them. As a result, Shamhazael and Azael both fathered the giants of the generation of the flood, who committed sins of adultery murder and robbery. Shamhazael even committed adultery with Ham's wife, who gave birth to Sichon, the giant, while she was still in Noah's ark. To cover his wife's shame, Ham had sexual intercourse with her, even though every creature was strictly prohibited to do so while in the ark.

In the Zohar, the Bnei Ha Elohim are treated as sons of the powerful. According to the *Zohar (Bereshith 37a)*:

> Rabbi Jose said: "When the descendants of Cain spread throughout the world, they used to cut up the soil, and they had traits in common both with the upper and the lower beings". Rabbi Isaac said "When Uzza and Azael (not to be confused with the Angels of the same name), descendants of Cain, fell from the abode of their sanctity above, they saw the daughters of mankind had sinned with them and begat children. These were the Nephilim or giants – *Genesis 6: 4*. Rabbi Hiya said "The descendants of Cain were the "sons of G-d" (*Ibid.2.*) For Cain was born from Samael and his aspect was not like that of human beings, and all who came from his stock were called "sons of G-d."

Rabbi Simeon Ben Johai once wrote that those who translate "Bnei Ha Elohim" as "sons of G-d" are in error, and should, in fact be cursed. The rendering of Bnei Ha Elohim in *Genesis* should therefore be "sons of the mighty". The Bnei Elohim, associated with the Archangel Raphael, should not be confused with the Bnei Ha Elohim, as their name does not have the definite article "Ha", nor are they the descendants of Cain, but Angels of the purest type.

Psalms 29:1, and 89:7, also make reference to the "sons of might," in Hebrew, Bnei Elim, which is yet another name given to the Bnei Elohim. "Ascribe unto the Lord, O ye sons of might..." Here, these Angelic hosts are invoked to join the earthly chorus in acknowledging G-d's majesty, as revealed in the mighty forces of nature. Even though these Angels were of great strength and might, they were still able to aspire to great spiritual and lofty heights by showing their more gentle nature in singing praises to the Almighty.

In *Job 1:6*, the Bnei Ha Elohim (here they seem to have added the definitive article "Ha") present themselves before the Lord who proudly shows off His servant, Job. What is unusual here is that Satan is among the Bnei Ha Elohim, and seems to have the role of Celestial Intelligence Officer, reporting to G-d in the Heavenly council. From this it is implied that the Bnei Ha Elohim are the supernal beings who are appointed to watch the actions of mankind when judged on New Year's day.

Further on in *Job 38:7*, we read, "When the morning stars (this is a reference to Angels) sing together and the Bnei Elim shout for Joy" (here the author has dropped the definitive article "Ha"). The question may be asked as to whether these Bnei Elim are the same as the Bnei Ha Elohim, for the verse implies that these are the same Angels of Judgment, who shout for joy as long as night continues, but who, when the stars set, give way to a new morning where Grace is awakened in the lower world.

As his name implies, Raphael is the Healer of G-d (more correctly translated as "G-d has healed"). He furnishes Man with a dwelling place, and through him the earth and Man are healed. Raphael was one of the three Angels *(Yoma 37a)* who visited Abraham in *Genesis 18: 2*. It was he who saved Lot when the city of Sodom was destroyed.

Genesis 5 begins, "This is the book of the generations of Adam..." In the Zohar, *Bereshith 55b*, we learn that the book referred to here was the same book originally given to Adam by the Almighty via Ratziel, the Archangel in charge of the Holy Mysteries.

When Adam transgressed the command of God, the book flew away from him. Adam then beat his breast, repented, and immersed himself up to his neck in the river Gihon. This made his face haggard, and his body became wrinkled all over. In his mercy, the Lord made a sign to the Archangel Raphael to return the book to Adam, who studied it for the rest of his life.

It is also said that the Archangel gave Noah a book of Healing, very likely the Sepher Ratziel, and it is Raphael who is said to be the preceptor of the patriarch Isaac. Raphael is credited as being the Angel who healed Abraham of the pain of circumcision. He also cured Jacob's thigh which had been wounded when he wrestled with the adversary, the Archangel Samael.

THE ARCHANGEL MEDITATION

The following is a well used Kabalistic meditation using 4 Archangels:

When all is quiet, sit peacefully and comfortably in a hard backed chair with feet and knees together and your hands on your laps. Close your eyes and relax. Visualize the Archangel Michael on your right side. He is the Prince and protector of Israel and all who believe in the one true G-d. Feel Michael so close to your right cheek that you start to have a warm tingling sensation there.

Still bearing Michael in mind, visualize the Archangel Gabriel, the Strength of G-d, on your left side. Like the experience with Michael, you now feel Gabriel's presence so close that both cheeks begin to tingle with a warm pleasant sensation.

Without opening your eyes "look" upwards and in front of you. You will "see" a strong light. This is the Archangel Uriel who is the Prince of the Light of Wisdom and Understanding.

Stay in this mode for a short while and bearing the three previous-mentioned Archangels in mind feel the presence of the Archangel Raphael, who has spread his healing wings around you and has also encompassed the other three Archangels.

At this juncture concentrate on all those who are ill and in need of Perfect Healing [Refuah Shlemah] and sense that healing pass from Raphael to them.

Once this has been accomplished envisage the Shechina, the holy Presence of G-d, hovering above you. Remain seated for a while and you will discover how relaxed and fresh this meditation makes you feel.

Gabriel - Cherubim

Yesod, which means Foundation, was produced by the union of the seventh and eighth Sephirot. In charge of this, the ninth Sephira, is the Archangel Gabriel, under whose wings are the Cherubim.

We read in *Ezekiel 9:3* that the "Glory of the Lord was gone up from the Cherub". According to Talmudic tradition (*Rosh Ha Shanah 31a*), the seat of the Shechina rested in the Holy of Holies, above the ark cover, between two Cherubim *(Numbers 7: 89)*. The reason why only one Cherub is mentioned in *Ezekiel* is that before Jerusalem was invaded and the first temple destroyed, the departure of the Divine Presence occurred in ten stages.

The first three stages were from the Ark cover to the first Cherub and from there to the second Cherub, which is the particular Cherub referred to in *Ezekiel 9:3*. The 4th stage is said to be "and the cloud filled the inner court" (*Ezekiel 10:3*)."And the glory of the Lord mounted up from the Cherub to the threshold" (*Ezekiel 10:4*) was the 5th stage. From the threshold the Shechina went back to the Cherubim [the 6th stage]. The Shechina then mounted the Merkavah, Chariot for the 7th stage *(Ezekiel 10:19)* and then for the 8th stage she, (the Shechina is feminine) stood at the East gate for a while [ibid]. It is interesting to note that when the Shechina finally returns to the temple *(Ezekiel 43:4)* it will enter through the same gate. The 9th and 10th stages were when the Shechina rested on the Mount of

Olives on the East side of Jerusalem for a full 3 ½ years (*Ezekiel 11:23*) in the hopes that the people would repent but they did not and so the Shechina parted.

In *Ezekiel 10:1*, the prophet no longer refers to the Angels of the Merkavah or Chariot Vision as Chaioth Ha Qodesh but as Cherubim. This apparent oversight is not in error, for this particular chapter deals with the Divine command to Gabriel ['the man clothed in linen'] to take coals from between the Cherubim and Ophanim, and set the now not-so-holy- Jerusalem ablaze. The rest of the Chapter deals with a renewed, though slightly different, description of the Merkavah, and its departure with the Shechina. As the Divine presence started the first phase of its departure with two Cherubim, it is only fitting that the last phase should end with Cherubim in control of the Merkavah or Divine Chariot *(Ezekiel 10:18)*. As previously stated, the Merkavah rested on the Mount of Olives for three and a half years, in the hope that the people of Israel would repent of their sinfulness.

In his description of the final rebuilding of the temple (which would usher in the Messianic Age), *Ezekiel 41:18* describes the wooden panels of the temple as being covered from the floor to the ceiling with Cherubim and palm trees as in the first temple of King Solomon *1Kings 6:29*. Each Cherub would have two faces - that of a man on the one side, and a young lion on the other. The two faces of each Cherub were to be turned in opposite directions, so that a palm tree would be between the human face of one Cherub and the lion's face of the other.

The reference to the King of Tyre, in *Ezekiel 28:14-15*, as a "Far covering Cherub", is merely the prophet's manner of describing the king as a great protector, a man who was perfect in his ways until iniquity was found in him because he became immensely wealthy, corrupt and conceited. Both the tabernacle and King Solomon's Temple depicted Cherubim with outstretched wings, symbolizing protection. As Tyre was described as the "Garden of G-d", its ruler, the king, was its natural protector.

Moses is commanded in *Exodus 25:18-20* to instruct the children of Israel to forge two Cherubim of beaten gold at either end of the Ark cover:

And the Cherubim shall spread their wings on high, screening the Ark-cover with their wings, with their faces one to another; towards the ark-cover shall the Faces of the Cherubim be.

Since Cherubs wore child-like faces, the mystical symbolism of these verses not only signifies the protective influence of G-d's Angels, but also the manner in which we should educate our children. Children should be taught to aspire upwards, just as the Cherubim spread their wings heavenwards. We should also teach our children to learn to protect the Ark of the Covenant and what it stands for. Our children should always be proud to face their fellow man, but at the same time, they should in all humility, turn their eyes to the Mercy-seat of G-d and only do that which is righteousness.

The Archangel of the Cherubim, Gabriel, is mentioned more than any other Archangel of the Bible. So great an influence is he that all three Monotheistic Religions acknowledge him.

Several references to Gabriel appear in the book of Daniel. In its powerful polemic against idolatry, *Daniel 3* teaches us that one should always be ready to suffer martyrdom for one's faith. The chapter depicts Daniel's friends Shadrach, Meshach and Abed-nego as being absolutely prepared to be cast into a fiery furnace, rather than serve the king's gods. In verse 24, Nebuchadnezzar, the king, is alarmed at seeing a fourth man, whereas only three men had originally been cast into the flames. The *Talmud (Pessachim 118a,b)* claims that this fourth man was none other than the Archangel Gabriel. The king describes Gabriel's appearance as being like that of the sons of gods; in other words, a Heavenly Being or Angel, so described, because Angels have free access to the heavenly abode, just as children have free entry into their father's house.

It is interesting that, although he admitted to the miracle of seeing an Angel deliver Daniel's companions from certain death, and even recognized Judaism as the true religion providing royal protection for its followers, Nebuchadnezzar did not institute the worship of G-d for all his people, nor did he himself convert. Instead he issued a decree making it a crime to even speak against the Jewish religion on pain of being cut into pieces.

There is a parallel in *Daniel 6* which deals with the well known story of Daniel in the lion's den [*verse 16*]. By his own decree, the new king, Darius, is reluctantly forced to cast Daniel into the lion's den, where G-d's Angel, on this occasion it was Michael, shuts the mouths of the lions so as not to harm Daniel. The king appears as a true friend of Daniel throughout the chapter. In *verse 18*, one would even call King Darius a true believer, but in verse 26, the king issues a decree which does not make the Jewish religion supplant all local forms of worship, but rather proclaims that the G-d of Israel should be treated as a Living G-d, whose dominion is everlasting. The king could not make the Jewish religion the only religion in the land because he himself was worshipped as a living god and this action would diminish his power in the eyes of his people.

In *Daniel 4:5*, King Nebuchadnezzar has a dream in which he again sees Angels, this time describing them as "Watchers" and "Holy Ones". The word "Watcher" is mentioned several times in the book of *Enoch*, although Daniel uses the term "Holy Ones" more frequently.

The Midrash tells of the time when King Nimrod ordered Abraham to be seized and cast into a flaming cauldron for refusing to worship the king. Gabriel begged the Lord that he should be chosen to save the patriarch from the flames. The Almighty answered him by saying, "There is none in heaven like Me, and on Earth there is no one like Avram. Therefore I shall descend Myself to save him from the fire". The wood in the oven then bore fruit, and sustained Abraham for three days.

The "certain man" in *Genesis 37:15*, who found Joseph wandering in the field in search of his brothers, is believed to have been Gabriel.

Later in the Bible, Gabriel is first mentioned by name in *Daniel 8:16*, where the Archangel is commanded, by a voice, to interpret Daniel's vision which foretold the future and its importance to world destiny. Some sources maintain that the future referred to here is the time of the Maccabees, while the more widely accepted understanding is that it is the Messianic Age.

It seems that Gabriel frequently helped Daniel in interpreting dreams. The Archangel is the "night vision" referred to in *Daniel 2:19* : "Then was the secret revealed unto Daniel in a vision of the night". By this vision, Daniel was able to tell Nebuchadnezzar both his dream and its interpretation.

The Archangel, who traditionally stands on the left hand side of the Almighty, while Michael stands on His Right, appeared a second time to *Daniel (9:21)*. [For Gabriel's first appearance see *Daniel 8:16*.] This time, Gabriel's task was to give Daniel a clear understanding of his first vision which left him so perplexed and which gave him a revelation of the coming of the Messiah, the Prince.

Once again, in *Daniel 10:5*, the "man clothed in linen", in his vision by the river Hiddekel, is the Archangel Gabriel. In the vision, Gabriel informs Daniel that the former had been delayed because the Archangel of the Persians had engaged him in battle for the past 21 days. Fortunately, the Archangel Michael, Patron Angel of Israel, had come to the rescue, and Gabriel was thus able to tell Daniel what will happen to his people at the end of days.

We learn from the Zohar *(Shemoth 11b)* that Gabriel is summoned by the Holy One each time a righteous person is born into this world. The Archangel transports the soul from paradise to the body on earth, and becomes its Guardian Angel. The name "Laila" is sometimes given to Gabriel, the Archangel of the souls of the righteous. There should be no confusion, since Laila means night. Gabriel comes from the "Left Side", and like all who come from that side, Gabriel also bears the name signifying "night". A further reference to the Archangel being of nocturnal habits is mentioned in *Daniel 9:21*, where Gabriel approaches Daniel "about the time of the evening offering." This reference to the evening offering implies the time when the evening sacrifice was offered in the Temple every day at twilight. *(Numbers 28:4)*

When Jacob blessed his sons on his death bed, his blessing to Reuben *(Genesis 49:4)*, "Unstable as water, have thou not the excellency..." is interpreted in the Zohar *(Vayehi 23 5b)* in the following way: Since the eldest son, Reuben, had tried to assert his chieftainship by sleeping with his father's concubine, none of his descendants would become rulers, kings or judges over Israel. In fact, they would not inherit inside the land, but they were cast out across the River Jordan. In his mercy, G-d appointed Gabriel to guard over the borders of the tribe of Reuben.

In the narration of the birth of Moses, in *Exodus 2:1-2*, the Zohar maintains that Amram, the father of Moses, had been "separated" from his wife Yocheved.

It was the Archangel Gabriel who brought them together again so that Moses could be conceived. The Midrash goes on to relate that Batya, the daughter of Pharaoh, was suffering from leprosy. Accompanied by her handmaidens, she had come to the Nile to cleanse herself. Seeing the child, Moses, in the bulrushes, the princess stretched out to save him. Her handmaidens loudly protested the transgression of the law in saving the Hebrew child, and especially at the hand of Pharaoh's daughter.

According to the Midrash, Gabriel was immediately summoned to strike the handmaidens dead, and to make Moses cry, so that Batya would have compassion on the child. As she stretched out her hand, it was miraculously cured of leprosy the moment she brought in the basket.

Gabriel came to Moses' rescue a second time when, according to Rabbinical legend, as a small child, Moses was put on Pharaoh's knee. Attracted to Pharaoh's shining crown, Moses took it and placed it on his own head. The court magicians, or astrologers, were horrified. Two braziers were immediately brought in. The one was filled with gold and the other with glowing coals. The astrologers counseled the king that, if Moses reached for the gold, it was obvious he was a usurper, and should be put to death. On the other hand, should the child reach for the glowing coals, it would be evident that, like all children, he reached indiscriminately for any glittering object. Moses instinctively stretched out for the gold, but Gabriel guided his hand to the coals. Taking up a burning coal, the child quickly put it to his lips, and for the rest of his life Moses remained "slow of speech and of a slow tongue" *(Exodus 4:10)* It was for this reason that Moses unsuccessfully argued with G-d at the burning bush not to send him to deliver the people from bondage.

The Midrash *(B'shalach)* informs us that, when the Children of Israel were walking through the parted Sea of Reeds, the Archangel Gabriel stood at their side, protecting them like a wall. To the waters on the right he proclaimed, "Guard the Israelites well for they will receive the Lord's Torah from his right hand." The admonition to the waters on the left was, "Harm not this people who will in the future lay tefillin, (phylacteries) on their left arms".

Sandalphon - Ishim

The tenth and final Sephira is Malchut (Kingdom). The Ishim rule in this domain, under their leader, the Archangel Sandalphon. Paradoxically composed of snow and fire, the Ishim are said to be the beautiful, or perfected, souls of righteous men. Their main function is to extol the Lord, and sing his praises. In his Mishnah Torah, Maimonides refers to the Ishim as a high order of Angels because he maintained that these Angels were originally the souls of righteous men.

According to Merkavah tradition, Sandalphon is the Keter or Crown of the Asiyatic or physical world. He is also the Tiferet or Beauty of the Yetziratic world, or world of Formation. As such, the Archangel not only corresponds to the Self of Man, but to the level of the Manifest Messiah. Sandalphon watches over the Crown of the physical body and the Beauty of the psychologically unawakened natural Man. When Man begins to evolve spiritually, Sandalphon lays the foundation to Man's "soul personality" and guards him through its evolution, until it reaches ultimate perfection. In the Zohar, Sandalphon is said to be the Archangel in charge of the birds, and is also called "Sar ha Ofot" –The Prince of the Birds.

Sandalphon skillfully fashions mystical crowns for his creator which, according to tradition, are made from Israel's prayers. Not only is he called the mediator between Israel and the Almighty (*Midrash Konen*), but he also has the power to nullify hostile decrees against the people of Israel.

The etymology of the name Sandalphon is "synadelphos" which means colleague, and many scholars therefore suggest that Sandalphon and the Archangel Metatron are colleagues, or even twin brothers. This is curious since Sandalphon is said to stand so far above his colleague, Metatron, that a journey between them would take 500 years. In the same manner that Metatron was proclaimed to be the transfiguration of Enoch, so too is Sandalphon described by many Kabbalists as being the Angelic transfiguration of the Prophet Elijah.

Spanish Kabbalists of the 13th century interpreted the name Sandalphon as "Sandal", meaning a still unformed embryo, and "Fon" (a derivative of the word "Panim"), meaning face. The two parts of the Angel's name represent the two elements, matter and form, which are brought together in him. As a result of this interpretation, Sandalphon is also called the Angel of the Embryo, and is thus seen as being instrumental in influencing the differentiation of sex in the embryo.

Another interesting interpretation of Sandalphon is that the word "Sandal" also has the meaning of "shoe" and that Sandalphon was therefore the "Shoe" of the Shechina, or more correctly, the Angel on whom the Shechina rested. While some mystics say that Sandalphon was the teacher of the prophet Moses, others consider him to be a special type of mystical being (none other than the transfiguration of Elijah), who was far more than simply another Archangel. Along with this school of thought, go all the many post-biblical, beautiful legends surrounding the prophet Elijah. To this day, Jews consider Elijah as being present as the chief guest at all ritual circumcisions for he is also called the Angel of Circumcision. Some go as far as to say that if a woman is barren and cannot bear children, after the ceremony, she should, sit on the symbolic Chair of Elijah, known as Kiseh Eliyahu, which is always present at these circumcisions. It is believed that if she does so she will fall pregnant within the year.

Most legends about Elijah, such as the following one, always contain a moral:

There was once a righteous man called Reb Shmuel ben Yosef who prayed to the Almighty to grant him the wisdom to understand the ways of the Lord. He prayed and fasted imploring the Almighty to help him meet Elijah whom he hoped would be able to enlighten him. To his great amazement Reb Shmuel finally did meet Elijah who asked him what he wanted. When Reb Shmuel told him that all he required was to accompany Elijah on one of his many journeys so that he could better understand the ways of the world, Elijah granted him his wish but on one condition. The pious Reb Shmuel would have to accompany him as a quiet observer and would not be able to ask any questions or Elijah would leave him immediately. Reb Shmuel agreed and without further delay the two set off on their long journey.

Their first stop was at a small run-down cottage owned by an elderly man and his wife. Their only possession was a cow from the sale of whose milk they barely eked out a living. This did not stop the old couple from making the weary travelers feel comfortable as they shared their meagre evening meal together. Elijah and Reb Shmuel kept their hosts enthralled all evening with their vast knowledge and interesting anecdotes. Early the next morning, as the two travelers were leaving, Reb Shmuel noticed Elijah giving a sign and instantly the couple's only cow died. Reb Shmuel was shocked, but before he could even protest, Elijah reminded him of the conditions under which Reb Shmuel was allowed to accompany him.

They journeyed on and at eventide Elijah decided to knock on the door of a local rich merchant's house. The servant who opened the door had already been instructed by the master of the house to escort the travelers to the servants' quarters but not to offer any food or drink. Weary and hungry the two men lay on the floor and eventually went to sleep.

At day break the next morning Elijah awoke his companion, but before leaving Elijah noticed a large tree that had recently been uprooted by a storm. With a quick signal from Elijah, the fallen tree straightened itself up and showed no signs of former distress, in fact its roots were even deeper and the leaves greener than they had ever previously been. Reb Shmuel once again restrained himself from complaining and continued the journey even more puzzled than before.

Having journeyed for yet another full day, Reb Shmuel accompanied his illustrious leader to a synagogue in the next town. As he entered he noticed the seats were lavishly inlayed with silver and gold. Not one member of the congregation stood up to greet or even escort the strangers to their seats nor did anyone invite them for dinner as is the custom in most synagogues. When the service ended Elijah and Reb Shmuel slept on the hard benches situated at the very back of the synagogue for they had nowhere else to go.

The following morning Elijah greeted the congregants as they entered the synagogue with the words "May the Almighty make you all Leaders." The congregants thought this was a great complement and the remark further confounded Reb Shmuel.

The travelers left immediately after the morning service and finally after a long journey arrived in another synagogue that evening. This time the congregants were poor but everyone welcomed them and offered them food and drink and warm beds in which to sleep. The following morning Elijah blessed the congregation with the words "May the Almighty bless you with only one leader." With that they left.

As they journeyed on, Reb Shmuel could no longer restrain himself for he had too many questions to ask of Elijah. "Enough!" he wept, "I very well know that if I ask you, you will leave me, I must know and understand what you have been doing because I really do not comprehend your strange actions at all. It seems that you have been rewarding those who do not deserve it and punishing those who merit better!"

Realizing Reb Shmuel's predicament and sincerity Elijah explained it all, "As for the old couple whose cow died, the wife was destined to die that day so I pleaded with the Almighty to instruct the Angel of Death to take the cow in her place. The tree that I straightened at the house of the wealthy merchant had a vast treasure hidden beneath its roots. The merchant's greed did not merit so enormous a fortune so I decided to hide it from him and I straightened the tree and reinforced its roots. With regards to the rich but selfish congregants whom I wished for many leaders, it was really a curse. It stands to reason that any group that is governed by many leaders is doomed to failure. Each leader will think that he is better than the next and therefore they will never agree to anything. My blessing to the poor but hospitable community to only have one leader was because it is better to have one wise man rule a city than a group of fools. Before we leave each other know this – when you see a wicked man prosper, you can be sure that in the end his wickedness will work against him. Conversely when you see a poor person undergoing what seems to be unfair hardship, you can be certain that they are actually being saved from something worse. Always remember that no one can understand the ways of the Almighty!"

With that Elijah departed leaving Reb Shmuel both a wiser and happier man.

Guardian Angels

It has been stated in a previous chapter, that Angels are guardians of the Sephirotic functions assigned to them. It is, therefore, quite natural to accept the concept of Guardian Angels in terms of individual experience. The Talmud states that no fewer than 11 000 Angels attend a person throughout his lifetime. Many people have experienced or sensed watchers over their lives.

The Zohar suggests that each one of us has a Guardian Angel assigned to us. Sometimes, the Angel may be relieved of his duties and replaced by another. One often senses this temporary stage between Angels, by feeling incompetent or suffering from the loss of a great 'companion,' even though no live friend has passed away. It is only through meditation that we can regain contact with our Guardian Angels, who not only work through the psyche of individuals, but also through the psyche of groups of people.

A GUARDIAN ANGEL MEDITATION

An excellent meditation for contacting your personal Guardian Angel is as follows:

Sit comfortably in a straight backed chair with your feet together and your hands facing downwards on your laps. Close your eyes and be aware of your breathing and at the same time allow your body to go limp and relax completely. Now think of nothing but emptying your thoughts. Do not dwell on any particular thought but cast it out of your mind as it occurs. Think of just being and not doing. First concentrate on all those you know who are suffering from ill health or a lack of peace of mind. Send them thoughts of good will, good health and peace. Now visualize what you wish to communicate to your Guardian Angel and remain passive and receptive. At first you will feel a warm tingling sensation. Above all you will feel at peace and when you open your eyes, you will feel a sense of accomplishment and relaxation. This meditation is well worth trying.

The Zohar also states that we are assigned two Guardian Angels at birth. The one angel is of the left grade (evil inclination), while the other belongs to that of the right (the side of righteousness). From the age of thirteen, one is given Free Will. If one chooses to walk in the ways of truth and righteousness, one has the assistance of the Angel on the right. Whatever good deed one performs, one enlists the aid of both Angels who will bring benefits, not only to the one who does good, but also to the rest of mankind. Should one elect to give more power to the Evil Prompter and go towards the left, not being circumspect enough to perform deeds in such a way as to benefit mankind, then one sinks lower and lower to that evil grade, until even the Angel of the Right leaves one's side.

To emphasize the need of doing good deeds, the Zohar goes on to tell us that for every good deed one performs, one creates a 'good' angel, and conversely, for every bad deed, an Angel of the side of the left is created. By the time one dies each 'good' Angel counteracts a 'bad' Angel until there is a surplus of either 'good' Angels or Angels of the evil inclination.

If there is a surfeit of good Angels, one is immediately escorted to the Supreme Judge by these Angels. Woe to the man whose bad deeds have created an excess of Angels of the left side, for they will torment him in Gehinom. His only salvation then is true repentance.

There is a very old and lovely story about a man who once dreamt that he was walking along the sea shore on a clear, cool evening. As the gentle moon came out and painted the sea with its silvery rays, the man sensed that he was no longer alone. He turned to find none other than his Guardian Angel at his side.

The two walked the lonely stretch of white beach for many miles together. As they journeyed, the man's life unfolded before him, and he relived both the many happy, as well as the numerous trying times of his past. At last, the man turned to his Guardian Angel and said, "Good kind sir, while we have been walking, I have often looked back in the direction from whence we came. I noticed that, as my life unfolded before me, and I experienced the good times, there were two sets of footprints. However, when the bad times were at hand, and I looked back, I could only find one set of footprints emblazoned in the sand. Why did you leave me when I needed you most?'
Came the Guardian Angel's gentle but firm reply, "Not so, my friend. When you needed me, I carried you in my arms, and that is why you saw but one set of footprints."

Another interesting (and somewhat amusing) tale is that of a man, we shall call him Moshe, who was so poor that he and his wife could not even afford having a child. Moshe always went around with a positive attitude knowing full well that the Almighty would one day ameliorate his situation. After all, he thought, is not the first commandment "Be Fruitful"!

One day Moshe's mother became totally blind and although he could not afford it, he brought his hapless mother to his house so that he and his wife could attend to her needs. One day in desperation Moshe prayed from his very soul and suddenly his Guardian Angel appeared. "Moshe," called the Guardian Angel, "The Almighty has heard your prayer and will grant you but one wish. Think hard on what you wish for it may turn out to be a mistake rather than a blessing. So I will give you a full week in which to decide." Moshe knew exactly what he wanted – riches – but before he could say so the Angel disappeared.

Moshe ran to his wife to tell her what had transpired and his wife chastised him for only thinking of himself. She reminded him how desperately they had always wanted a child. Full of guilt poor Moshe turned to his mother who further added fuel to the fire by reminding him of her own needs.

For a full week Moshe prayed for enlightenment and when finally his Guardian Angel appeared and asked him what was his wish, Moshe replied "Good kind Sir, I ask not for myself but only that my dear blind mother will soon see her grand child in a golden carriage."

There are many reports of individuals who have narrowly escaped death by what should have been a fatal accident. They will swear that a dearly departed, husband or relative, had come to their rescue in the guise of a Guardian Angel. True, their Guardian Angel, did, in all probability, come to their rescue. The fact is that everything happened so quickly, and at that particular split second, their minds were probably turned towards their departed loved one. They thus mistook the Guardian Angel's identity for that of their loved one. Besides, their loved one was more than likely undergoing a period of transition before the next reincarnation and therefore could not possibly have been there. Another explanation is that a Guardian Angel can only manifest himself in human form and therefore takes on the likeness of a particular departed person.

It is believed that Guardian Angels are spiritual beings assigned to aid us in many different ways. We find at many stages that our lives are being intercepted by certain "powers" that seem to assist us and make our lives run more smoothly. This can occur by a sudden thought of inspiration coming from nowhere that spurs us on or even by giving us superhuman strength as for example in the case of a man being able to lift up a car long enough to save his wife who is trapped beneath it. In fact there are many recorded cases that are often explained as luck, coincidence or sometimes even a miracle.

We might well then ask, why do Guardian Angels only assist us at certain times and not every time that aid or succor is needed or asked for; and why do Guardian Angels assist some people and not others. Man is a free agent and although they give loving and caring support, Guardian Angels must often stand back while man out of necessity works things out for himself.

After all "G-d helps those who help themselves." Guardian Angels are always willing to come to our aid, or even communicate with us but all too often we are just too busy to listen and that is the reason why some people report an "experience" while others seem to have had no contact at all.

Guardian Angels not only protect individuals, but are also set over whole nations. The Zohar (*Waera 30b*) reiterates the words of the Torah, informing us that there are no fewer than seventy Guardian Angels who guard the nations of the earth. Later rabbinic writings cite only four nations that are guarded:

Persia, whose Guardian Angel is Dobiel, Edom (later the Roman Empire), is guarded by Samael, Uzza, the Guardian of Egypt, while Israel has Michael as its Patron Angel.

Although it does not mention each Guardian Angel by name, we are told in the book of *Daniel 10:21* that the "Prince" or Guardian Angel of Israel is Michael. According to the Midrash, Egypt was guarded by Uzza who pleaded for his people not to be annihilated at the parting of the Red Sea [the Sea of Reeds]. The Almighty held a celestial tribunal of all the seventy Guardian Angels to see whether the Egyptians deserved to perish. Uzza eloquently pleaded with the Almighty, saying, "Master of the Universe, the Truth lies with you, and so does Justice. Could you not save the Israelites without destroying the Egyptians?" With that, the Archangel Michael motioned to Gabriel, who swiftly flew to Egypt. Gabriel soon returned with a brick into which a Hebrew child had been cemented. With this "evidence", the Attribute of Justice turned to the Lord, and asked him to execute Judgment upon the Egyptians, for they were guilty.

The Guardian Angel of the Amalekites was none other than the Angel of Death (Samael), who was the Guardian Angel of Esau. It is Samael who fought Jacob and was defeated. Esau's descendants, the Amalekites, swore vengeance on their patriarch, and waged war on the Israelites at Rephidim, but they lost, and now no longer exist. Nevertheless, the threat of the Amalekites persists. In the words of the law giver, Moses, "The Lord will have war with Amalek from generation to generation" *(Exodus 17:16)*. Courage, conviction, truth and righteousness remain the only true weapons in the continuous battle against the spirit of Amalek, the force of evil, which to this day, still stalks the earth.

Angels of the Months and Planets

Sepher Yetzira, the Book of Formation, is considered one of the earliest books on the Kabala and its contents are traditionally believed to have been handed down by the Patriarch Abraham. As with many ancient writings, there are many versions but only four of them have emerged as the most acceptable. They are: the Short Version, the Long Version, the Saadia Version and the Gra Version. According to the Gra version, Angels exert their influence, although only in a purely guardian role, over the months of the year as well as the twelve constellations.

The Hebrew calendar is based on the moon's phases and therefore does not coincide with the Gregorian calendar which is presently universally accepted.

The Month of Nisan which usually falls between March and April is guarded by Samael while the sign Aries has Uriel as its guardian.

The month of Iyar, equivalent to April/May has Aniel as it's guardian with Imriel guarding the sign of Taurus.

Sivan, falling between May-June, has the angel Gansharish as its guardian while Tzafaniel guards the sign of Gemini.

Tamuz, corresponds to June-July and is guarded by Cadniel with Tariel guarding the sign of Cancer.

Av which usually falls between July and August is guarded by Tzidkiel. Barakiel is in charge of the constellation Leo.

Elul, corresponding to August-September, is protected by Akhniel and Paniel is in charge of the sign of Virgo.

Barakiel is the custodian of the month of Tishrei, which falls between September and October. The sign of Libra has Tzuriel as its guardian Angel.

The month of Cheshvan corresponds to October and November and its guardian is Ismariel while Kabriel is the Angel who protects the sign of Scorpio.

Kislev corresponds to November-December and is protected by the archangel Gabriel. Adniel is the custodian of the sign of Sagittarius.

Tevet equivalent to December-January is again guarded by the Archangel Gabriel. Tzafiel is the keeper of the sign of Capricorn.

The month of Shevat corresponds to January-February and is protected by the Archangel Uriel. The Angel Yariel is the guardian of the sign of Aquarius.

The month of Adar corresponds to February-March and is guarded by the Angel Berakhiel. The sign, Pisces has Sumiel as its guardian.

From the above it will be noted that certain Angels, such as Gabriel and Barakiel, have been given more than one month or planet to guard. Considering the fact that only one Angel can perform one duty at a time; one can only surmise that where an Angel has two functions to perform they are not done simultaneously but are given to the next Angel in the hierarchy of their Order. This is, however not quite true. Named Angels, especially Archangels, are given the privilege of multi-tasking.

Western astrology assigns the positions of the signs of the Zodiac to the position of the sun, whereas it can be noted from the above that, according to the Kabala a more precise allocation is through the twelve Hebrew lunar months. Therefore this latter method is considered more accurate. It is interesting to note that in Judaism it has generally been forbidden to draw pictures of the figures that represent the signs of the Zodiac because in ancient times this practice led to the worship of the signs as gods. It is, however, permitted to draw the stars and join them together by lines and dots and thus create the emerging patterns. We are admonished not to make astrology a dominant influence in our lives, for we are taught to put our faith in G-d alone.

If Angels can guard the months it is only natural to assume that they are also guardians of each day that passes by. According to *Sepher Yetzira 4:14* the following Angels govern the days of the week:

Sunday: Semeturia, Gezeriel, Ve'enael, Lemuel

Monday: Shmaiyel, Berekhiel, Ahaniel

Tuesday: Chaniel, Lahadiel, Machniel

Wednesday: Chizkiel, Rahitiel, Kidashiel

Thursday: Shmuaiel, Ra'umiel, Kuniel

Friday: Shimushiel, Raphael, Kidushiel

Saturday: Tzuriel, Ratziel, Yofiel

Being guardians of the months, days and the signs of the Zodiac, it follows that Angels are also guardians of the seven planets that can been seen with the naked eye and channel their influence accordingly. Many variations are given as to what planet is governed by which Angel. So as not to cause more confusion the following is an accepted list found in Sepher Ratziel 17b (51):

Saturn-Michael. Jupiter-Barakiel. Mars-Gabriel.

Sun-Raphael. Venus-Chasdiel. Mercury-Tzidkiel.

Moon-Anel.

The Talmud [Hagiga 14a and Moreh Nevuchim 2:6] states "Every word emanating from G-d creates an Angel." From this we learn that every word from the Almighty actually brings about the creation of an Angel. G-d's word is His interaction with the lower worlds and this force that travels across the spiritual world is known to us as an Angel. We also learn that the Almighty's providence works through the Angels who in turn work through the stars and planets. This makes the Angels seem almost like souls to the stars and it is for this reason that some sources consider the stars as having intelligence but it is actually the Angels who operate through the stars that have that intelligence.

Taking into consideration that each of G-d's words create a new Angel, some authorities claim that new Angels are created each day and they even state that whole myriads of Angels are created each morning. This leads us to the thought that, resultantly, there must be two different types of Angels. They are the Angels that are created every day and are temporary and nameless, whereas those Angels who were created on the fifth day, the same day as the birds were brought into this world, are permanent and have names such as Gabriel, Michael etc.

We are told that the Angel, Lailah, who is in charge of all births proclaims whether the new born will be strong or weak, rich or poor, wise or foolish. It would seem that he has many missions to perform. This begs the question as to whether this Angel is breaking the rule that only one task can be given to one Angel at any one time and moreover that two Angels cannot share the same task.

The answer is quite simple when one realizes that Angels are like souls to the stars. We know that humans have souls which are spiritual entities with each soul being integrated by its connection to its body. It is obvious that all humans can multi-task without restrictions or the necessity of having other bodies or other souls. So, too, the Angels that have names, being souls to the stars, can perform many tasks because each star serves as the focal point for each Angel maintaining it as an integrated whole.

There is a one-on-one relationship between star and Angel. Each star has its own Angel and vice versa. It is this association between star and Angel that allows each named Angel to perform many tasks.

When speaking of the stars, *Isaiah 40:26* states "He brings out their host by number, He calls them all by name." By this we are told that each star has a name and it stands to reason that each named Angel was created on the fifth day after the stars had been created on the fourth day.

Reincarnation

No book on Angels would really be complete without referring to reincarnation and the important role that Angels play in reincarnation. To more fully comprehend this we must first understand exactly what reincarnation is.

Many opinions exist about reincarnation and just as many sources will negate any or all of these theories. There is an opinion held by many religious leaders that reincarnation will only occur "at the end of days" when the Messiah will come and all those that have previously died will suddenly come back to life as in Ezekiel's vision of the dry bones [*Ezekiel* 37:1]. In fact Ezekiel's manifestation is really a graphic vision of the rebirth of the nation of Israel given to inspire the despairing Jewish exiles. It promised that a restored and invigorated people of Israel would eventually return to their home land never to be uprooted from their soil and, as in verse 25, "They shall dwell therein, they and their children, and their children's children for ever; and David My servant shall be their prince for ever." Ezekiel was not referring to any final resurrection or even to reincarnation but to the founding of a new State of Israel.

If the premise that all the dead since creation will reincarnate at the time of the advent of the Messiah were true, just imagine the population explosion! True, it has been prophesied that the dead will come back to life at the time of the Messiah but the reference was intended to include only all those souls in a state of transition. Meaning those having not quite finished their soul cycle and are waiting to be reincarnated at that particular time.

Assuming that life is only about being born, slaving away to make ends meet, raising a family, dying and then waiting to be resurrected, life would have little or no purpose at all. A widely accepted explanation of reincarnation is the one that is adhered to by most modern Kabalists who believe that we are reincarnated many times before we reach a state of not having to return to this plane again because we have reached a state of perfection. Some call it Cosmic Consciousness.

We are born into this world, or plane, for very specific reasons. Life is one big learning curve. In fact our main purpose in life is to learn certain lessons that are set before us.

An over simplified allegory would be as in the instance when teaching a child not to put his or her hand in the flame of a candle because it would burn. If the child does not learn this lesson he/she will continue to place his/her hand in the flame until it would finally sink in that a candle flame does hurt... And so it is with us. In life we are taught many lessons and if we do not learn them, we will reincarnate many times until we finally do.

Reincarnation is a natural phenomenon and like all natural phenomena, reincarnation must, of necessity follow a cycle. One school of thought maintains that this cycle lasts, approximately, one hundred and forty four years. But in Mysticism nothing is written in stone because a cycle could be far less. If one wishes to go by this theory one takes one's birth date and then calculates one hundred and forty four years backwards arriving at a certain period or date in history. It must be born in mind that one then has to add upwards of fifteen years (some are satisfied with taking their present age) to arrive at a time when one would be able to function then as an adult given the fact that the average life span was far less than it is now. Once one has arrived at that date one should consult the internet or a book on history of the world and one will immediately be drawn to a particular country whose history will seem most familiar.

We know that the cycle of reincarnation begins at birth. Genesis 2:7 states "And the Lord, G-d formed man of the dust of the ground, and breathed into his nostrils the breath of life; and man became a living soul". This means that our souls do not return to this plane and enter our bodies until we take our first breath of air at the time of being born. When we die and exhale our last breath, our souls return to G-d from whence they came.

On entering into this life we are born close-fisted signifying that as we get older we are obsessed by material possessions, but when we die, we die with our hands open showing that we leave all behind and take nothing with us.

Contrary to popular belief we do not go straight to heaven or hell when we die. What happens is our souls leave our bodies and we enter into a state of transition. A guardian Angel, some call it a hidden Master, takes over as our instructor. Just as in a television series we are given a review of our past lives and a preview of the next incarnation. The Angel will go to every length describing where we went wrong and how we should have improved the situation. Our Angelic instructor further shows us where the pitfalls of our next life will be and how we should overcome them.

The Zohar tells us that just before we are ready to reincarnate our Angel will place its [Angels do not have a sex] index finger on our lips as a sign that we should not reveal what we have learnt. The Zohar goes on to say that that is the reason why we all have an indentation between the nose and upper lip. Just before all this the soul is given the opportunity to actually choose its new parents. Often we hear children telling their parents "Well its not my fault, I did not ask to be born!" In fact they did ask and they did choose the parents that they wanted before entering this plane.

This begs the question as to why does one not remember all the foregoing. The answer is quite simple. Considering the fact that most of us can only recall very few instances when we were say five years old, and those we do recall are probably because we have been told about them by our parents. How then can we expect to remember everything that happened, even say one hundred years ago?

Skeptics will ask how does one prove all this? The answers are obvious. We have already mentioned above that a simple method is to go back in time and one is bound to find a period in history that intrigues us the most because one actually lived through that time. Others will tell us that dèja vu, the experience of being in a certain place that is familiar even though we have never been there before, or even meeting a person for the first time that we would swear that we have met before [probably in a previous life] is simple proof enough. It is said that when we dream of far off lands and speak the language of that particular country, we are in fact actually speaking that language because it is the same as that of when we were there in a previous reincarnation.

On the subject of dèja vu, we are told that should we go on a journey and happen to sit next to a person whom we have never met it is destiny that we have been placed together because of the reincarnation forces that are in play. We have the option of either not making verbal conversation at all, but should we choose to speak to these people we will find that we learn much from them or become very friendly and possibly even keep in constant contact with each other after the journey. Often we make friends with these people that we knew in a previous life and it is our duty to carry on where we ended previously.

A better way to find out what we were in a previous incarnation is through meditation and the following Magen David Meditation has been proven to be most inspiring:

MAGEN DAVID MEDITATION

Sit on a straight backed chair with your knees together, your feet on the floor and your hands comfortably placed facing downwards upon your laps. With your eyes closed picture in your mind's eye a beautifully manicured lush green lawn upon which is a path in the shape of a Star of David, or Magen David.

Walk slowly upon that path and make your way to the uppermost or furthest point of the Magen David. Once there you will find that straight ahead of you is a lovely field studded with many wild flowers of almost incandescent hues. As you traverse the field, you look ahead and realize that there is a mountain at the far end of the field and as you approach it you make out the entrance to a cave.

Make your way to the entrance of the cave and as you enter the cave you are somewhat surprised to find that instead of darkness you are greeted by light because the walls are brilliantly lit up. Approach any wall and place your hand upon it. Instead of the wall being solid you find that your hand is able to go right through it. Follow your hand and you will find that your whole body is able to get to the other side where you will discover many scenes from a previous reincarnation.

You may do this meditation as many times as you wish and each time that you do, you will encounter new scenes. One should always bear in mind that the real reason for wanting to do this exercise is not out of pure vanity or curiosity, but its purpose is to analyze where one went wrong in a previous reincarnation and whether one has fallen into the same bad habits as in that previous incarnation. Moreover one must ask whether one is still following a similar pattern and if so, how must one try and figure out what is the best path to take in order to improve one's life.

It has already been stated above that the reincarnation cycle is not always one hundred and forty four years. Let us take the case of when a person who is very family oriented dies at the same time that there is a woman in the same family who is pregnant and she decides that she will call her baby after the dearly departed. The soul of the departed will be tempted to reincarnate into the baby especially if the latter is given his/her name not withstanding the short period that has lapsed since the death of that particular person. It is imperative that parents choose the name of their children wisely. Sometimes the person after whom the child is named, was not such a savory character after all and the unfortunate child will display those same characteristics in adulthood.

In some recorded cases parents cannot understand why their baby seems to have an affliction, such as, for example, a limp, when no physical evidence or cause can be medically presented. On further reflection the parents might remember that the person whose name their child carries walked with a limp. It is only by meditation, prayers and changing the child's name that the child will "miraculously" return to a normal condition.

A soul has a great affinity to enter a body and there are many recorded cases when, for example, a man undergoes a serious life threatening operation and is declared clinically dead but inexplicably comes back to life. Often it is because the man in question actually died and another soul has now inhabited his body. The wife of the first man will notice that although her husband still looks the same he has developed certain new character traits, either for better or for worse, and she will even tell her husband that he is a different person than he was before the operation. Usually neither party understands exactly what has transpired.

On the other hand, because mankind is gifted with free will, not all of us return after the one hundred and forty four year cycle has expired. Many will opt out and not wish to be reincarnated into a world that is filled with hunger, disease and strife. Those that do skip a reincarnation or two will do so until they find that this is to the detriment of their own progress.

We often wonder why bad things happen to good people or why some people are very rich and take cruel advantage of the poor. The rich seem to wax richer while the poor continue to suffer. We are told not to question the ways of the Lord but to continuously praise him because we will never understand His ways. The rich man who has taken advantage of the poor will surely get his just deserts either in the next incarnation or at the very end of his present incarnation. This is where the Divine Law comes into play (some call it Karma).

Whatever we do in this reincarnation will definitely have certain repercussions in our next. If we lead a life of righteousness we will reap the rewards either in the present or in a future reincarnation conversely if we lead wayward lives and no matter how outwardly it may seem that we can get away with it, our punishment will surely be meted out in the next reincarnation.

It is said that the good die young and one often asks, "why does a very young child die so young?" The answer is quite simple. The child has actually reached perfection in the previous life and comes back for two main reasons: either to look around this plane for one last time, but more so to teach a lesson to his/her loved ones or even the people whose lives that young person may have touched. Whether the loved ones have learnt the lesson or not all depends on their having fully understood the purpose of the life of the departed.

Our souls are divine but the moment they enter the human body they become encrusted with our wrong doing because "there is no man who has walked the earth and who has not sinned." Every time we do wrong we add another husk and it should be our life's aim to endeavor to remove these husks by bettering the way we live, by doing good, giving charity and leading exemplary lives. There is no such thing as soul devolution, our soul personalities are ever striving for perfection. They may even skip several rungs in the ladder of soul evolution in one lifetime in order to achieve perfection. A soul may come into this incarnation as a woman and then as a man in its next reincarnation, but it always comes back as a human being and not an insect or animal as is believed in certain cults and religions.

Let us examine the case of incorrigible souls who are serial killers or who murder every time they are incarnated and who never seem to be able to learn the lesson that to kill is unacceptable. At first these are given several chances to improve and are reincarnated a number of times.

Eventually when all fails they are prevented from being reincarnated any further. Some authorities say that their souls are incarcerated into a stone or tree in a far remote area where they remain until they repent. It is for that reason that these same sources state that one should never remove stones or chop down trees from remote areas. Other authorities insist that these hapless souls go straight to hell, wherever that place may be.

It is said that marriages are made in heaven and that soul mates are joined together at that time. The Zohar tells us that when G-d first created souls he formed them into male and female pairs. Does this mean that we marry the same soul mate every time? This idea poses many questions. For instance what happens when a couple divorces and each partner remarries? In Lurianic Kabala we are told that the original primordial soul contained 613 limbs and each limb contained 600 000 smaller roots and when multiplied it gives us more than 2 000 trillion possibilities of soul mates.

A more acceptable explanation is that when we reincarnate we may enter into the body of a baby with a different sex to what we had in the previous incarnation. Our original soul mate may now very well be of the same sex as we are. Eventually, if we are fortunate we will encounter our original soul mate but in the mean time we must look upon our spouses as heavenly given and therefore we must appreciate and cherish that gift.

Similarly, when a couple with children divorce and remarry, often to a spouse that makes them far happier than in the previous marriage. Usually it was destined that these children of the previous marriage had "chosen" their parents, for it was their destiny to have that particular set of parents' D.N.A and character traits. As for the next couples' marriage or marriages, in all probability they have now found their true soul mates.

A question that is often asked is whether the Angel that is assigned to us during transition eventually becomes our Guardian Angel once we reincarnate into our next life. As previously mentioned, there are no hard and fast rules. Certain Angels are assigned specific tasks and if an Angel's work is to deal with souls in transition then it is safe to assume that it alone is their assigned task.

Guardian Angels are allocated to us to guide us through life, but a specific Guardian Angel can and will change and possibly will be given to another person to whom the way is shown. That is when we sometimes feel that we are all alone in this world with no one to turn to. This is mainly because we are between the "change of the guard," so to speak. We do, however, revert to our more positive selves once a new Guardian Angel takes over.

We often find that when a friend has lost a loved one, it is immediately assumed that the departed soul is now in Heaven. Signs like the flickering of a candle or the inexplicable dimming of a light are taken for granted as signs that the loved one is now an Angel in Heaven and is sending a "sign". We also hear of cases where a woman has recently lost a husband and is involved in a car accident. She will swear that her husband came to her in the guise of an Angel and told her to jump away from the car minutes before it explodes into fire. True, a Guardian Angel would very well have been responsible for warning her, but unless her husband was a perfected soul, he would still be in a state of transition or even have reincarnated into another body. But it is not for us to spoil her belief especially if she is happy in that thought.

Angels play a tremendous part in reincarnation, in transition and in our present lives. It is up to us to appreciate them and be able to work with them in bettering not only our own lives but the lives of our fellow man.

Demons

Much has been written about Demons and although far more literature exists on Angels both are subjected to many sources of information and unfortunately with just as many conflicting points of view.

Demons are the ubiquitous antithesis of Angels. They are surrounded by ancient mythology and medieval superstitions. In fact if more of us would concentrate our thoughts on the positive good and less on the negative evil of demons, the world would be a far better place in which to live with far fewer demons.

Demons are created by humans. Every time we entertain an evil thought or carry out an evil deed a new demon is created. Some sources go as far as to say that sin is promulgated at the moment when it is first thought about and not afterwards, whether the evil deed is actually performed or not. The thought counts.

Many view demons as creatures that are something between Angels and Man. They have wings, are shape shifters and move with great speed foretelling the future so that later they will be able to gain trust and convince Man only to deceive him later. Like humans, demons can eat and drink, have sex, propagate and die. Because they do not have real bodies they are unable to cast shadows and they can only have sex with humans in dreams or on a non physical plane.

Other sources say that it is the human imagination alone that gives birth to demons.

Even the Talmud tells us that demons can be overpowered by humans and goes on to relate a tale of the wise and learned Rabbi Abaye who was once confronted by the queen of the demons, Agrath. She foolishly told him that he was immune from her powers because Heaven had granted him impunity on account of the fact that he was so wise. Grasping at the opportunity the Rabbi put a hex on her, banishing her from populated areas. And that is why some are convinced that one can still find demons in dark and narrow alleyways.

It is widely believed that demons, I prefer the phrase evil spirits, lurk in cemeteries. One should always return home from the cemetery on a completely different route to the one that one had taken to arrive there. This is supposed to confound the evil spirits who originally followed one to the grave side. It is also necessary to wash one's hands and give charity before leaving the cemetery for this will ritually cleanse one of any evil spirits and the act of charity will counteract any power that the evil spirit may wish to extend.

Once captured, Demons can be put into the service of Man to do only good things as illustrated in one of the many legends about King Solomon. The Archangel Michael once gave King Solomon a ring with the fantastic powers of subjugating demons. With the help of certain Angels that had the power over demons, King Solomon was able to capture the demon Asmodeus, who originally was a Persian rather than a Jewish demon, but nevertheless was incorporated into Jewish folklore as an evil spirit. Asmodeus taught the king the secret of the "Shamir," a worm that could split rock. The Shamir was used because no metal tool was allowed to be employed in the Temple during its construction. *1 Kings 5:17* tells it differently: The stones used in the construction of the Temple were hewn off site and then brought "...to lay the foundation of the house..."

The story is purely allegorical for it could not be possible that demons were used to build the first temple, the most holy site in the history of the Jewish people. It merely illustrates that the demons of our thoughts can be put to good use if we choose to have the power over them. Conversely if we allow demons to have power over us our lives can be made wretched and seemingly without purpose.

The Archangel Samael (see chapter on Samael) is the prince of demons and is also known as Satan, the "Adversary", who "stood up against Israel, and provoked David to number Israel" (*1 Chronicles 21:1*). Now it was permissible to number Israel only after having received the explicit command of G-d. This injunction is taken from *Numbers 1:1; 3:14 and 26:1*. No one actually physically counted each person but the method used was that each person donated half a shekel as in *Exodus 33:12* "As a ransom for his soul." The coins were then counted and their sum signified the number of people that there were.

Joab, the captain of David's army warned David against the census but the king's word was law and it prevailed. As a result of the census G-d cursed the Israelites with a plague. Realizing that it was his fault King David summoned the prophet Gad who told him that he could choose three years of famine, three months in which the enemy would sweep him off his feet, or three days in which the Angel of the Lord would smite the land with a plague and destroy many of its cities. Just as the Destroying Angel, some say it was Uriel, was about to destroy Jerusalem the Lord repented and ordered the Angel to cease.

According to certain sources the Angels of Destruction live in the nether region but can only do G-d's bidding. It is also said that these same Angels of Destruction assisted the Egyptian magicians in turning their staffs into snakes and turning water into blood in order to discredit Moses in the eyes of Pharaoh.

Some mystics will argue that Demons actually do exist. Whenever we feel that we are experiencing serious problems and our lives are literally falling apart, we attract demons that are relentless in their fiendish actions. Other mystics are more comforting in their explanation. They believe that demons are the evil qualities which we find within ourselves. They will tempt us to do demonic deeds but just as in the story of King David, we do have the free will to ward off these nefarious actions. Especially comforting is the knowledge that if we truly repent as David did the Lord will be compassionate in dealing with us.

Epilogue

Our journey has brought us through the mystical portals of the Ten Sephirot. We have seen that each Sephira is governed by an Archangel, and the particular order of Angels over which he rules. It is hoped the explanations presented in this book have provided the reader with a clearer picture as to who Angels are, as well as their specific functions. In the final analysis, we see Angels are exactly what their name implies - messengers.

Especially over the past two millennia, Angels have mistakenly been regarded as having supernatural powers, and as being divided into two camps; the forces of good or light, and the forces of evil or darkness. Being the Almighty's messengers, Angels can only do G-d's bidding, and cannot take matters into their own hands. Even Samael, or Satan, is restricted to doing that which is the will of the Almighty, and within the Divine Scheme of things. After all, the Almighty created all Angels to do His Bidding. In modern times, many unenlightened people have accredited Satan with more power than he actually has. Hell is what we make of our own lives, and Satan has as much control of our lives as we wish to believe or allow him to influence us. In addition to their role as messengers of the Almighty, Angels are also guardians. The Talmud tells us that "every blade of grass has over it an Angel saying 'grow'". Perhaps their most important function is to act as G-d' s choristers, and constantly sing His Praises.

Man should aspire to be like the Holy Order of Ishim, who bear his name (Ish means Man). For, through righteousness, and constantly praising the Almighty, Man can create Heaven right here on earth.

Bibliography

The Soncino Books of the Bible edited by the Rev Dr.A.Cohen.
The Soncino Press
London. 1968

The Zohar Translated by Harry Sperling and Maurice Simon.
The Soncino Press .
London. 1956

The Kabbalah Unveiled translated by S.L. MacGregor Mathers. Routledge & Kegan Paul
London. 1968

Understanding Jewish Mysticism by David R. Blumenthal. Ktav Publishing House.
New York. 1978

The Midrash Says by Rabbi Moshe Wissman. Bnei Yakov Publications.
New York. 1980

The Holy Scriptures according to the Masoretic text. The Menorah Press
Chicago. 1973

Sepher Yetzirah. The Book of Creation by Aryeh Kaplan.
Weiser Books Boston MA. 1997

The Bahir by Aryeh Kaplan.
Weiser Books Boston MA. 1998

About the Author

Norman Naim Amato was born in Gatooma Rhodesia (now Kadoma Zimbabwe). As a teenager and later as a young man he came under the influence of Rabbi Dr. M. Papo PhD who became his mentor in many Kabalistic teachings.

Norman has taught Kabala for many years both in Zimbabwe and North America. He is currently the Grand Master of The Order of King Solomon's Kabalistic Knights for North America.

www.ingramcontent.com/pod-product-compliance
Ingram Content Group UK Ltd.
Pitfield, Milton Keynes, MK11 3LW, UK
UKHW020139250726
13967UKWH00002B/755

9 781425 138530